# Understanding Your Loved One's Eating Disorder and How You Can Help

why she feels fat

{ JOHANNA MARIE MCSHANE, PhD &
TONY PAULSON, PhD }

Why She Feels Fat
Understanding Your Loved One's Eating Disorder and How You Can Help

© 2008 by Johanna Marie McShane, PhD and Tony Paulson, PhD

Gürze Books
P.O. Box 2238
Carlsbad, CA 92018
(760) 434-7533
www.gurze.com

Cover design by Johnson Design

Library of Congress Cataloging-in-Publication Data

McShane, Johanna Marie.
  Why she feels fat : understanding your loved one's eating disorder and how you can help / Johanna Marie McShane & Tony Paulson.
    p. cm.
  Rev ed. of: Because she feels fat, 2004. iUniverse.
  ISBN-13: 978-0-936077-29-1
  ISBN-10: 0-936077-29-8
  1. Eating disorders. 2. Eating disorders--Patients--Family relationships. I. Paulson, Tony. II. Title.
  RC552.E18M42 2008
  616.85'26--dc22
                          2007049571

The authors and publishers of this book intend for this publication to provide accurate information. It is sold with the understanding that it is meant to complement, not substitute for, professional medical and/or psychological services.

The case studies in this book have been thoroughly disguised to preserve confidentiality; all names are fictitious.

3  5  7  9  10  8  6  4

# Contents

## PART III - SUPPORTING THEIR RECOVERY

# Acknowledgments

We would like to gratefully acknowledge all of those who participated in the creation of this book. We were honored and humbled by the courage demonstrated by those who shared their stories with us. Their candor and willingness to share their thoughts, feelings, and experiences allowed us access into the world of eating disorders and gave us insight into the tremendous suffering they experience. We would also like to acknowledge our families for their eternal patience and support throughout this process. Finally, we would like to thank our editor, Lindsey Hall Cohn, for her tireless effort and insight.

# Introduction

Eating disorders, such as anorexia and bulimia, are serious, life-threatening illnesses that impact not only the person directly suffering, but also her family and friends. They are perplexing, exasperating, and ultimately seem to make no sense whatsoever to those who desperately witness their loved ones wasting away.

However, the behaviors inherent to an eating disorder make great sense to the person involved; and, for the most part, she will be confused and annoyed that others seem incapable of understanding her perspective when it's so very clear: she "feels fat," therefore the obvious course of action is to either restrict what she eats or purge her body to rid herself of food. Why is that so hard to understand?

What may *not* be clear to all involved is that "feeling fat" is more about psychological pain than the size of her body. It also reflects a sincere desire to be accepted by a culture that glorifies impossibly thin bodies. For this reason, *decoding the deeper meaning of the statement "I feel fat" is at the heart of this book*, and is crucial for the person in recovery, as well as family, friends, and caregivers.

To that end, *Why She Feels Fat* defines and explores eating disorders "from the inside out" in an attempt to convey the emotional experiences and perspectives of those who have anorexia or bulimia. It is our deepest hope that by providing this intimately subjective view, you will feel empowered and confident during your loved one's recovery. The greater your understanding of these illnesses, the better able you will be to make informed decisions in all aspects of your loved one's care.

*Why She Feels Fat* is divided into three sections. The first introduces the diseases themselves: anorexia, bulimia, and the "grey area" termed Eating Disorder Not Otherwise Specified (EDNOS), which includes behaviors that do not fit exactly into the category of either anorexia or bulimia, but warrant attention nonetheless. It also discusses the common signs and symptoms of eating disorders, typical medical complications, and imparts current knowledge regarding underlying causes.

The second section focuses in detail on the subjective experiences of those who have eating disorders. These individuals possess unique perspectives about themselves, their bodies, and food. Despite the fact that you might consider their views to be inaccurate, bizarre, or irrational, they have a consistency and structure. *Why She Feels Fat* will help you truly comprehend how your loved one thinks and interprets the world at large. With this informed understanding comes the ability to better relate to her experiences and garner empathy and compassion rather than judgment and despair.

The final section explains what to do when you first discover your loved one has an eating disorder. Our step-by-step discussion will encourage and empower you to seek appropriate help. We offer and describe the many options for treatment, how long it will take, and what to expect from your loved one as well as yourself during the healing process.

Throughout the book are quotes from girls and women who have courageously offered to share their stories. Although they are not noted individually, we would like to acknowledge the important and selfless contribution they have made to this book. Their openness and willingness to share intimate details of their lives affords a unique opportunity for all to see the world through their eyes.

Please note that, although eating disorders affect both genders, we have chosen to use feminine pronouns throughout this book. Nonetheless, all concepts, experiences, and recommendations apply equally to males.

why she feels fat

**PART I**

{ *Understanding Their World* }

**CHAPTER 1**

# The Basics of Eating Disorders

## *Bingeing, Purging, Starving: What's the Difference?*

The term *eating disorders* incorporates a wide range of food, weight, and exercise-related behaviors (or *symptoms*). In terms of food and eating, these behaviors fall on a continuum encompassing everything from starving oneself, to bingeing and purging, to bingeing without purging. In terms of weight, the range is from severely underweight to markedly overweight. Perhaps the most well-known eating disorders are anorexia and bulimia, but many individuals suffer with debilitating symptoms that don't quite fit into either category.

At first glance, eating disorders appear to be all about food: your loved one says she wants to lose a few pounds or is trying to eat in a more healthy manner or get in shape. She may herself believe such statements, since these illnesses often start out as an attempt to "take better care" of oneself by starting a diet or exercise plan.

However, if we look *beyond* the specific behaviors, we find these disorders are actually methods of dealing with life. Even if your loved one only started out "to lose a couple of pounds," manipulating food or exercise soon becomes a way to help her feel secure and make her life more predictable. It also becomes a means of communicating emotions she can find no other way to express.

What's more, as the eating disorder begins to take hold, food, exercise, and weight develop increasingly intense emotional significance. Food is no longer just food. Rather, it takes on great symbolic meaning, synonymous with her value and worth as a person. Throughout this book we'll explain the process, why it makes sense to your loved one, and what you can do to help.

## *How Can Food Have Emotional Meaning?*

Think about the last time you picked up something to eat, say, a banana. You probably didn't think much about it, other than whether or not it was ripe. When someone with an eating disorder picks up a banana, however, her thoughts are more like, "How many calories are in this banana and if I eat it will I get fat?" or "Eating this banana will make me appear weak or out of control," or, "People would think I'm a pig if they saw me eating this!" The banana and what is done with it have enormous meaning.

*If I ate one bite my whole day was ruined. It changed everything. I could be feeling pretty good about myself, but as soon as I ate anything I thought I was a horrible person and that I shouldn't be allowed in public.*

*If I could throw up, things went back to normal. I felt like I was back on track, like I was acceptable in the world. If I couldn't throw up I felt like I was the worst person ever.*

*If I could go a day barely eating my life was organized. It all felt in place. I could stand anything that happened in my day, because I felt like I had it all under control. But if I had to eat, it all felt so chaotic, like I didn't know what to do, didn't know how to act, what to think, or what to expect. It felt terrible, totally out of control. So I'd do anything to get out of eating.*

*Purging got me back on schedule. It gave a structure to my day. If I ate without throwing up, I felt out of control all the time. Like I was free-falling.*

*I could say to myself, it's only a piece of toast. And I knew in my mind it couldn't hurt me. I'm not dumb. But somehow I still didn't believe it. I was just sure it had some power to destroy me, to take away everything that mattered to me.*

## Why Does She Need These Behaviors?

We all strive to feel secure and in charge of our lives. We're most comfortable if we have some level of structure and stability, and we do countless things on a daily basis to ensure that this is the case. For instance, we developed relationships that are fulfilling, and in which we can be honest about how we think and feel. We pursue careers that give meaning and financial stability to our lives. We take care of ourselves to keep healthy. These types of things allow us to anticipate what our experience will be like *most* of the time, and give us a concrete sense that we have the power to create the kind of life we want.

Your loved one approaches life with the same desire for structure and security. But the types of guidelines you use don't work for her, or she can't manage to create them for herself. So, she needs to find something else to rely upon. That's where the eating disorder comes in.

Her thoughts and beliefs about food illustrate how this works. For example, she may say to you, even a bit casually, "I don't much like cheese." But what she's *really* thinking to herself is something like, "cheese is a bad and dangerous food; therefore, as long as I avoid it, I'll be safe." In this context, it means she feels "safe" from becoming "fat." But in truth, her belief has little to do with cheese and almost everything to do with trying to understand, organize, and control her life. If you ask her to join you for lunch she may tell you she's already eaten, while saying to herself, "If I skip lunch I'll feel so much better." Again, on the surface she may believe she's declining your invitation to prevent "getting fat," but there is far deeper and more encompassing meaning to her actions. Because she is unable to create other types of principles to guide her, she turns to and regulates her thoughts and beliefs about food and weight to give her life structure and to feel safe. This idea is central to eating disorders.

It's crucial to remember that no one *decides* to have an eating disorder. Your loved one didn't wake up one day and think, "Oh, here's something that will make me feel secure!" Her dependence on the disorder has developed gradually, over time. In fact, she probably hasn't even noticed the progression from her being in control of her behaviors to the behaviors being in control of her.

> *I always thought I could stop whenever I wanted to. I'm strong and I have a lot of willpower. It was scary to see that I couldn't stop. I wasn't in control anymore.*

> *That's when I realized I needed help—when it was clear to me the eating disorder had its claws in me and there was nothing I could do to stop it.*

> *I thought I had everything under control. I don't know when I noticed, but somewhere along the line, I lost control. It had control over me, not me over it.*

If the idea of using food, weight, or exercise as a way of organizing life seems strange to you, you aren't alone. It's hard to make logical or rational sense of unfamiliar behaviors. But, to your loved one, they *do* make sense, a lot of sense, just as yours do to you. Recognizing, instead of judging, this fact is what's important.

Before we explore the experience of having an eating disorder, we'll identify some basic signs and symptoms.

# Anorexia Nervosa

A fundamental organizing principle for someone with anorexia nervosa is the belief that if she can be "thin enough" her life will be better. Her strategy to feel stable and secure is to avoid being fat.

> *As long as I stay thin, nothing bad will happen to me, and people will like me and never leave me.*

> *Being fat is terrifying. I don't even know why. I just know it is.*

> *I never worried about anything happening. I could handle anything, as long as I was thin. Nothing bothered me then. But if I felt fat, I knew I was weak, and I felt so vulnerable. I hated that feeling.*

> *Having to eat is a sign of weakness and failure.*

> *I can have complete control over what I eat. It's my way of showing my family that I'm good enough as a person.*

Not surprisingly, the central feature of anorexia is weight loss, which can occur rapidly or gradually and, when left unchecked, can become extreme and lead to death. Restricting food intake, or fasting altogether, and exercising excessively are the most common ways of achieving weight loss, but sometimes the individual will purge in some way in order to get rid of what she's ingested.

> *I throw up just about everything. It really depends on the type of day I'm having. I mean, sometimes I'll get rid of a cup of coffee.*

> *After I eat a certain amount, I have to go run. How long I run depends on what and how much of it I ate. Two hours is the minimum though. Any less than that won't get rid of anything.*

> *If I feel it in my stomach, I'm getting rid of it. It doesn't matter what it is, I'm getting rid of it. I can't stand to feel anything in my stomach.*

Anorexia often begins as a temporary diet and for this reason can seem relatively harmless at first. In the early stages, the individual usually feels invincible and "totally in charge" of her life. She might be proud that she can accomplish something (weight loss) that most people find hard to do. As the disease roots itself, she'll begin to passionately protect and defend her behavior. She won't want to change or give up what she's doing, and will fight ferociously to keep anyone from getting in the way of what she sees as her choice.

As the anorexia progresses, however, her sense of power and control begin to erode, and at some point, she'll likely begin to feel hopeless and helpless, and as if her life is chaotic. By this time, however, even if she's aware the disease has taken over her life, she is so dependent on restricting food and losing weight, and so afraid of what will happen if she changes anything, she'll most likely continue to defend her behavior.

Ritualistic behaviors regarding and eating food are commonplace in anorexia, and the individual may create many "rules" about the "acceptability" of a particular food or how it is prepared. She'll tend to be extremely picky about which foods she'll allow herself and will often eat in rigid and calculated ways.

> *I have to cut up anything I eat into an even number of pieces, usually 20 or 30. It's better if the number of pieces can be divided by 5; that makes it easier to eat. If the food isn't cut like this, I can't eat it.*

> *I won't eat after 4 p.m. I don't know why. Anything I eat after that will turn to fat.*

> *Whatever my family is eating, that's bad. I skip anything they're having for meals.*

> *Nothing white. White rice, white bread, white sugar, nothing. White as a food color is evil.*

## Being Thin vs. Feeling Thin

One of the most baffling characteristics of anorexia is the fact that your loved one can look in the mirror and truly *not* see that she's underweight. If you've ever tried to explain to her that she *really is thin*, you've probably noticed your efforts are typically ineffective and the interactions leave you both frustrated. However, she isn't lying about what she sees or feels about her body because an inherent aspect of anorexia is a distortion in perception that renders her unable to accurately and objectively view herself.

> I know other people look at me and see me as thin, but I don't. I don't feel thin. It's about how I feel. It's hard to explain. Sometimes I feel thin, but most of the time I don't.

> I can tell when I'm fat because my clothes don't fit like I want them to, or I feel my stomach sticking out. I just feel fat!

> I wish my parents would get off my back. They say I'm too small, but I know they are lying. They just want to make me fat.

> If anyone looked in the mirror and saw what I see, they'd starve themselves too.

> I always see fat. It doesn't matter what anyone else sees or thinks. I always see fat.

Body image distortion can affect people in a variety of ways. One person may see herself as too big overall, whereas another may focus on specific body parts.

> There isn't a part of me that isn't fat and disgusting. I'm an embarrassment.

> My arms are thin. Probably too thin. But my legs, and especially my butt, are just huge.

What other people else think about her body size is irrelevant to someone suffering from anorexia. The only thing she cares about is if *she* experiences herself as thin, which is primarily based on how she feels at a particular moment. This means that her perception of her weight and body can change, depending on other variable factors, such as whether people appear to like her that day, her score on a test, or if she does or does not eat lunch.

Satisfaction over the weight loss is usually short-lived, and she quickly begins to feel "not thin" at this new body size, forcing her to pursue further restriction. As she continues to become smaller, she may experience a sense of pride or strength based on her ability to withstand hunger, to deprive herself of food, and to resist other people's attempts to make her eat.

> *I remember walking into the cafeteria and looking at everyone eating lunch and thinking that I was somehow better than them. I mean, I was able to do something they weren't—not eat.*

> *It didn't matter what my parents said. They could try all they wanted to, but I wouldn't let them win. It was all about proving I was better than that. That I didn't have to eat.*

## Warning Signs of Anorexia Nervosa

- Preoccupation with weight
- Relentless drive to be thin
- Withdrawal from friends or group activities
- Preoccupation with food
- Irritability or mood swings
- Fear of particular foods
- Compulsive counting of calories or fat grams
- Intense fear of gaining weight
- Compulsive exercising
- Continued weight loss
- Lying about not eating
- Preoccupation with how food is prepared

- Obsessively reading cookbooks
- Low self-esteem
- Depression or thoughts of suicide
- Feelings of hopelessness
- Intense sensitivity to criticism
- Difficulty identifying physical or emotional feelings
- Frequently weighing herself
- Dissatisfaction with her body size and shape
- Irregular menstrual cycle or cessation of menstruation (amenorrhea)
- Perfectionist standards; high-achievement expectations
- Difficulty concentrating or thinking
- Denial about illness or about severity of illness
- Overconcern with what others think
- Growth of fine hair (lanugo) on arms, face, or back
- Rigid thoughts or behaviors
- Rituals with food
- Compulsive schedule-making
- Intense fear of failure

This is not a comprehensive list, and it's important to remember that exhibiting a single symptom does not mean someone has anorexia.

## Medical Complications of Anorexia Nervosa

Eating disorders can lead to serious, potentially fatal physical problems. An estimated 10–15 percent of individuals suffering from anorexia die as a direct result of their disease. The following are the most common medical consequences of anorexia:

- Weakening of the heart due to malnutrition (including potential heart failure)

- Low blood pressure
- Low body temperature
- Irregularities in, or loss of, menstruation
- Dehydration
- Electrolyte imbalance (essential minerals found in the blood)
- Anemia
- Gastrointestinal disturbances
- Osteoporosis
- Lowered immune system function/low resistance to infection
- Low blood sugar (hypoglycemia)
- Kidney impairment or failure

## Bulimia Nervosa

Someone with bulimia experiences conflicted and often agonizing feelings about food. Whereas the main goal of someone with anorexia is to avoid it at all costs, which is a relatively clear and consistent mandate, the intentions of someone with bulimia are more complicated and tumultuous.

*I have a love/hate relationship with food. I love it when I'm bingeing, and I hate it the minute I realize what I've done.*

A person with this disorder alternates between believing eating will make her feel better and thinking that food is something "poisonous" that must be eliminated as quickly as possible. This conflicted relationship is illustrated by the characteristic behavior of bulimia: episodes of binge eating, followed by purging to get rid of what was just eaten.

Like anorexia, bulimia often begins as an attempt to lose weight or "get healthy." And, like anorexia, it tends to be progressive.

*I only binged a few times. It seemed harmless enough. Then I started feeling fat and I taught myself how to purge. It was all downhill from there. I was addicted to it. Once I learned I could purge I went crazy with it all.*

*It seemed kind of gross at first, but then I got used to it. It didn't bother me after a while.*

*At first it was really hard to do. It took a long time and was kind of painful. But I kept at it, and then I got really good at it.*

*It started an activity I could do with friends. We all ate a lot on weekends, then we'd go back to our rooms. I don't know how many girls threw up, but I sure did. At some point I think most of my friends grew out of it. They sort of got bored or something. But not me. I just got more and more into it over time.*

The eating behaviors associated with bulimia tend to be cyclical and can be erratic. Your loved one may exclusively binge and then vomit. Some individuals binge and then excessively exercise, while others overeat and then restrict their food intake for several days afterward. Alternating periods of bingeing and purging with restricted dieting is not uncommon. Some individuals employ any combination of these and/or other behaviors. Regardless of specifics, the overall pattern is one of over-consuming immediately followed by some type of behavior to compensate.

## Bingeing

While bingeing used to be defined as the consumption of large amounts of food, or an "eating spree," clinicians now realize the term can mean different things to different people. In effect, what constitutes a binge depends upon the perspective of the person who is doing the eating, and the difference can be vast. For example, one person might describe a binge as consuming far larger quantities of food than she normally would during a typical meal, whereas another person may feel she has binged after eating a single piece of bread.

*I plan my binge all day. Then I go to the store and buy as much food as I can. I will buy gallons of ice cream, bags of cookies, and anything else I see. I eat until I am in so much pain that I can't eat any more. Then I purge.*

*Sometimes I can drink a glass of water and feel like I have binged. Then I have to go and throw it up.*

*One bite of anything sweet will do it. I don't care what it is, or what I've eaten all day.*

For an individual who has a healthy relationship with food, overeating focuses the attention on the discomfort of being overly full. It *heightens* an awareness of the physical state. For your loved one, though, bingeing *lessens* her connection to her body and emotions. It *diminishes* her awareness. In fact, this is the driving force behind bingeing.

*When I eat, I don't have to feel.*

*I forget about everything.*

*Time stands still. For that brief period, I don't have to worry.*

Being able to "numb out" is a relief. She can, for a short time, "escape from the world." But although it feels quite powerful at the time, bingeing doesn't actually solve any of her problems or fundamentally change any of the worries she wanted to avoid in the first place. The anesthetizing effects are fleeting and usually disappear as soon as she stops eating, or soon thereafter.

## Purging

Once this numbing effect wears off and she becomes aware of what has happened, the binger experiences an urgent need to "get rid of" the food. Typically, she will use self-induced vomiting, laxatives, diuretics (medicines designed to reduce or eliminate excess water in the body), emetics (medicines designed to induce vomiting), and/or excessive exercise to do this.

It's curious to note that, in some ways, the effects of purging are similar to those of bingeing. Purging promotes a numb feeling and distracts the individual from anxiety about her life in general. She has but one thought— to get rid of what she ate. Nothing else concerns her, no goal is higher on her list. But purging has some added "advantages." It can be a way to express anger (at herself or others), to punish herself for having been "bad" (by overeating), or as a way to redeem herself for having binged (which allows her to feel like she's a "good" person again).

*The way I purge feels aggressive. And that's how I want it. It feels like I'm releasing a lot of rage.*

*Purging is such a relief. I mean, physically, obviously, since I don't have a painful, bulging stomach, but also emotionally. It releases all my emotions.*

*After I throw up I feel like I can be a member of the human race again. Like I've atoned for my sin of bingeing.*

Although someone with bulimia can be as preoccupied with food, weight, fat, and calories as someone with anorexia, she doesn't usually suffer the same dramatic weight loss. More often than not she will have a relatively average body size, although her weight can fluctuate significantly. However, for those individuals with bulimia who are underweight, purging can be particularly dangerous, causing an increased risk of medical complications.

## Warning Signs of Bulimia Nervosa

- Bingeing
- Impulsive behavior (stealing, lying, risk-taking)
- Hoarding or stealing food
- Overuse of laxatives, diuretics (water pills), emetics (such as ipecac), diet pills
- Secretive eating
- Water retention
- Swollen glands
- Frequent trips to the bathroom, especially immediately after eating
- Low self-esteem

- Feelings of hopelessness
- Intense sensitivity to criticism
- Eating when not physically hungry
- Feelings of disgust or self-hatred
- Obsessive or compulsive behavior
- Difficulty identifying physical and emotional feelings
- Overly concerned with what others think
- Excessive exercise
- Perfectionist standards; high-achievement expectations
- Depression (can include suicidal thoughts or attempts)
- Irritability or mood swings
- Feelings of shame, guilt, embarrassment, or humiliation about eating behavior
- Dissatisfaction with body size and shape
- Change in social behavior (withdrawal or isolation)
- Feeling "out of control" (with regard to eating or other aspects of life)
- Weight fluctuations

## Medical Complications of Bulimia Nervosa

Fewer people die from bulimia than anorexia, and consequently the physical impact of this eating disorder is often ignored or minimized. Despite the lower death rate, people with bulimia can incur serious and even life-threatening medical problems, such as:

- Electrolyte imbalance (essential minerals found in blood)
- Menstrual irregularities
- Potential heart arrhythmia or irregularities (due to electrolyte imbalances)
- Esophageal bleeding or rupture

- Gastrointestinal dysfunction (such as ulceration, abdominal pain, bleeding, bloating, constipation, non-responsive bowels)
- Dehydration
- Osteoporosis
- Lowered immune system function/low resistance to infection
- Tooth decay

## Other Types of Eating Disorders

Many people suffer from significant problems with eating, weight, exercise, and body image that don't necessarily fit into the categories of anorexia or bulimia. Therefore a new and specific diagnostic category called Eating Disorder Not Otherwise Specified (EDNOS) was created to encompass the diversity of issues related to disordered eating.

Examples of individuals who have eating disorders that might be termed EDNOS are:

- Someone who has suddenly lost weight, has restrictive food behaviors, and has distorted thinking about her body, but has not lost the 15% of ideal body weight required for the clinical definition of anorexia.

- Someone who has suddenly lost weight, has restrictive food behaviors, and has distorted thinking about her body, but who has not lost her menstrual cycle.

- Someone who binges and purges less than the twice a week required for the definition of bulimia, or has purged for less than a total of three consecutive months.

- Someone who binges but doesn't purge afterward (often called "binge-eating disorder").

- Someone who repeatedly chews then spits out food to avoid swallowing it.

Ailments that fall into this category are often serious enough to warrant treatment and can be severe enough to cause great pain and suffering. Also, the behaviors of one disorder often overlap those of another, and they can change over time. For instance, it's not uncommon for someone to initially restrict food intake, but then replace this activity with bingeing and purging. If your loved one has symptoms even though they don't fit the precise definition of anorexia or bulimia, don't minimize the need for intervention.

When trying to establish whether your loved one has an eating disorder and whether or not to intervene, rather than attempting to determine which type, we find it useful to gauge the extent to which her behaviors are affecting her quality of life. If her food and exercise regimens are causing significant negative effects in any area, be they physical, emotional, social, or spiritual, then no matter what the specifics, she needs help.

**CHAPTER 2**

# The Causes of Eating Disorders

## *Why Did This Happen?*

A common explanation for the development of eating disorders is society's preoccupation with thinness, and this certainly plays a part. However, most clinicians believe that there are many other contributing factors, including psychological, social, familial, spiritual, and at times biological.

Many useful books discuss the causes of anorexia, bulimia, and related eating problems. However, our goal is to help you understand your loved one's *experience* and grasp why her behavior makes sense to her. Therefore, in this chapter we briefly discuss causes, and only in general terms.

### Cultural Factors

In our culture, both men and women are pressured to look a certain way. Men are encouraged to be big and muscular with little or no body fat. Women are led to believe they should be thin. Although it has not always been the case, a person's value is often associated with their size and/or shape. Consequently many of us base our own feelings of success or worth on the extent to which we conform to society's idea of the "perfect" body.

## Men and Being "Buff"

A few decades ago, a popular magazine advertisement depicted a cartoon showing a thin, pale young man who was desperate to become "buff" so he'd be admired by his girlfriend and respected by the muscled men he saw on the beach. The product promised to make him big and powerful, clearly delineating a connection between body size and being a worthy, vital man.

Our society's current version of the ideal male body is "cut," "lean," and "ripped." This "perfection" has a very narrow definition, one that few men are physically able to achieve through a healthy diet and exercise. In response, some develop anorexia nervosa in an attempt to lose all body fat. Others develop a relatively new phenomenon termed "reverse anorexia," a condition in which the individual sees himself as physically underweight and weak, no matter what his true body size. As a result, he goes to great, if not extreme, lengths to become more muscular, often putting his health and life at risk.

## Women and Being Thin

For women, a thinner, less curvy "ideal" shape has replaced the once-admired hourglass figure that was popular for centuries. This trend toward thinness was exacerbated in the 1960s when 17-year-old British model Leslie Hornby, nicknamed *Twiggy*, met with unprecedented popularity in the UK and America. At that time she stood 5' 7", had measurements of 31-22-32 inches, and weighed only 97 pounds.

It wasn't long before girls and women alike began patterning their makeup, hair, clothing, and body shape after hers. Thinness became associated with success, wealth, beauty, and power. The myth that being thin is a requirement for a happy life found a new and eager audience.

Conversely, as our culture has come to *overvalue* thinness, it has also come to *devalue* any body shape considered too big. Women with larger bodies are often viewed as weaker or less intelligent than their svelte counterparts. They are disregarded for certain types of jobs, thought to have poor social skills or fulfilling relationships, and "billed" as lonely, deprived of affection, and overly dependent on others. These false beliefs persist despite the fact that there's no evidence that such things have anything whatsoever to do with body shape or size.

Our personal attitudes and stereotypes about body size and what it implies don't just suddenly appear one day. They tend to form and develop when we are young, and typically become more established as we mature, sewing the seeds of body dissatisfaction that eventually grow into eating disorders.

*I was very overweight and I got teased. I was so lonely and always felt left out. No one wanted to be my friend. I decided early on that I'd better not stay fat.*

*My family made fun of fat people. All of us did. It was like a sport for us. Now I'm ashamed of how we acted. But it did drive home to us kids that being large was not something good to be, not something to be proud of.*

*My mom was big, and she hated it. She talked about it all the time. I decided early on that I'd never let that happen to me.*

*My whole childhood I heard, "You'll never make anything of yourself if you grow up fat."*

No matter what they do, most women aren't physically capable of reaching the degree of thinness portrayed as ideal in our culture. Nonetheless, many will spend their lives attempting to alter their bodies and feeling inadequate and dissatisfied with themselves as a result.

## Physical Changes Due to Puberty

Both girls and boys experience normal, dramatic, physical changes related to puberty, and females specifically must increase body fat in order for menstruation to begin. Many young women do not know this fact, and begin dieting or resort to an eating disorder in response to this normal biological change.

> *I suddenly started growing taller really fast. My body didn't feel like my own. After a while I got used to the new me, sort of like I grew into my new size.*

> *Nobody told me what was supposed to happen in your teenage years, about what my body needed to be doing. So I fought it. My friends all did too. We thought we had things wrong with us. I wish someone would have told us what to expect.*

> *I gained weight in places I had never had weight before. My mom explained that that was because my period was coming. I was nervous about it, but she turned out to be right.*

## Personality Characteristics

Just as people in general are unique and varied, individuals who develop eating disorders encompass a diverse range of personality types. They can be shy or gregarious, introverted or extroverted. They may enjoy many hobbies or only a few. They can love to go to parties and be social, or prefer to stay at home alone or with just a close friend.

This being said, individuals who are prone to developing eating disorders often share specific personality characteristics. They tend to be perfectionists, highly-driven, and ambitious. They can also be anxious or "high-strung" by nature, as well as sensitive, inclined to "people pleasing," and self-doubting about their thoughts, opinions, and beliefs.

> *I care too much about what everyone thinks about me. I want to make everyone happy all the time. I don't care how that makes me feel.*

*People always say how compulsive I am. How driven I am all the time. But I can't sit still. I have to be moving and doing things all the time.*

*I've always been fear-based. I'm afraid of everything. Especially change. Even good kinds of changes terrify me. I hate being so insecure.*

*Everything has to be in its place. If it's not, I get so nervous I can't stand it.*

Insecurity is a constant theme for someone with an eating disorder. She may worry a great deal about whether she's good enough, whether she's loved, whether she's making the "right" choices. She may feel she isn't as smart, competent, or powerful as other people.

*I don't know what I'm doing. I never know. Why is it that everyone always seems to know what to do? How do they know?*

*I second-guess myself like crazy. I'll think I think one thing, then the next minute change my mind. Again and again, over and over. Whatever anyone's opinion is, that's what my opinion becomes.*

*I'm afraid people won't like me if I do the wrong thing. I'm terrified about not making the correct choice or decision.*

This low self-esteem and lack of confidence are often perplexing to friends and family. Their perception is that she's a capable individual and they expect her to have a strong sense of who she is, high self-esteem, and great self-confidence.

## Biology

Many individuals who suffer from eating disorders also suffer from depression or anxiety. Some research has suggested that particular types of brain chemicals, called *neurotransmitters*, may be involved.

For instance, disturbances in amounts of the neurotransmitter serotonin might be responsible for some of the bingeing and purging behaviors of bulimia. Serotonin may also be involved in the regulation of hunger and fullness. Individuals with anorexia often have lower-than-normal levels of another neurotransmitter, *norepinephrine*, which is believed to be partly responsible for regulating mood, alertness, and response to stress.

One of the difficulties in deciphering a biological component in eating disorders is determining whether an imbalance in neurotransmitters precipitates the development of the illness or whether the imbalance occurs as a *result* of the disorder. This depends on the individual and is best discussed with a medical professional.

Genetics may also be a factor. Research in this area has been initiated in part by the observation that anorexia can run in families, and that bulimia repeatedly occurs in families where members suffer from depression or alcoholism. Many questions about the relationship between genetics and eating disorders remain to be answered and deserve additional study.

## Family

Significant attention has been paid to the family dynamics of people with eating disorders. Unfortunately, trying to understand the influence of close family relationships sometimes leads to blaming others, particularly parents, for their perceived failures or shortcomings. To do so is neither helpful nor particularly accurate. Our experience has been that, in general, families have good intentions and try to do the very best they can.

That said, some shared characteristics exist in families where an eating disorder is present, and becoming aware of them is useful. One commonality is that they tend to have difficulty expressing and managing emotions, something that can be due to a number of factors. For this reason, helping families learn how to handle their feelings in an effective and healthy way is a critical aspect of recovery.

> *My family doesn't know what to do with feelings. We just pretend they don't exist. I don't know what to do with them either, so I throw them up.*

*In my family you always had to act pretty. You could never be mad or loud.
You could never make noise. I learned to not show what I was really feeling.
Sometimes I'm still not even sure what I'm feeling.*

*My father was really volatile. He could get really mad and yell. I hated it. It
felt so unsafe and out of control. I hate that I could have feelings in me that
might be scary and out of control.*

Also, in some cases the quality of the bonds between family members is
lacking. Instead of being flexible, respectful and balanced, where each
person involved feels freedom to be him or herself, the relationships tend
to fall into three general categories: too close (enmeshed), too distant (dis-
connected), or an erratic combination of the two.

*My mom always wanted me with her. It felt like she wanted me to be her
best friend. It felt creepy to me. I wasn't her friend, I was her daughter.*

*My family's relationships are inconsistent. They change from minute to
minute. It feels crazy. You never know what to expect.*

*I love my sister, but she acts like she hates me. Most of the time she gives me
the silent treatment, she won't say a word. We live in the same house, but
we may as well be a million miles away.*

*I missed my dad a lot. He traveled a lot for work and even when he was
there I didn't see him. I guess since he was gone so much, even when he was
home, my mom managed everything. She didn't let him really parent us. He
got more and more distant over time. I wondered if he felt left out. I sure felt
left out from him.*

## Changing Parental Roles

As children mature, assume more independence, and take on added re-
sponsibilities, the role of the parents continually shifts. In general, the
younger their ages, the more parents are involved in decisions regarding
their children's lives.

But an important aspect of growing up is learning to make one's own choices. Stepping back and allowing children to assess their options and make their own choices may be difficult, but doing so is essential to their healthy development.

In families where an eating disorder is present, however, parents commonly have difficulty with this issue. One family, for example, may worry that their child isn't ready or able to make the "right" choices for herself, so instead of encouraging her to take on this challenge, they continue to make decisions for her. Another might expect their child to be capable of making decisions that are far beyond what's appropriate for her age or abilities, and therefore choose to remain distant and comparatively uninvolved. Yet another family may show signs of both of these attitudes, if, for instance, the parents have conflicting ideas about child rearing. Regardless of the situation, the end result is invariably the same: confusion on the part of the loved one, and trouble or failure when she tries to consider options and then choose what she believes to be best *for her.*

*It was hard for my mom to trust me. She worried and worried. But after a while she could see that I didn't always make "perfect" choices, but I mostly did okay.*

*My folks acted like they thought I as 25 when I was 11. They had me set my own curfew, buy my own groceries, choose most things for myself. Then they wondered why I didn't make the "right" choices. Hello, I was 11— I didn't know what I was doing.*

## Overwhelming Events

An eating disorder can also be precipitated by a situation or occurrence that feels overwhelming or traumatic. Although the exact nature of the event isn't as important as how it is experienced by your loved one, triggers include: leaving home for the first time (summer camp, college); the death of a parent; verbal, emotional, or sexual abuse; or teasing and bullying.

*A group of girls at middle-school started harassing me—about everything.*

*They were just plain mean. I was terrified of them. And I wanted to disappear.*

*I thought I was really independent and grown up. I couldn't wait to go to college. But once I got there, I really didn't know how to take care of myself at all.*

*My brother got mugged in the city. He was okay, but the whole thing freaked me out. It made everything seem so random, so out of control.*

## Determining a Cause

The cause of an eating disorder is quite a bit more complicated than, say, that of a bacterial infection, which can be directly traced to the presence of a particular organism. With an eating disorder, though, several factors are usually involved, and no two cases are exactly alike.

Sometimes it is more useful to think in terms of *risk factors* that might predispose someone to the development of the illness. One person can have every possible risk factor for an eating disorder and remain perfectly healthy. Someone else may have only one, but because of the particular constellation of events that make up her life and how they affect her, she may go on to develop full-blown anorexia or bulimia.

Although the idea of discovering what underlies your loved one's illness may be tempting, try not to place too much value on the emergence of a simple, single cause. Exactly what happened to precipitate the eating disorder may never become clear, and dwelling on this issue too long or too much can become burdensome and frustrating for everyone. Remind yourself that what *is* important is how to treat the disorder once it's been recognized.

**CHAPTER 3**

# Beyond the Symptoms

## *What Do Her Behaviors Mean?*

Acquainting yourself with information about the symptoms of eating disorders is essential. Knowing warning signs and what to look for allows you to keep an eye out for potential trouble. At the same time, though, they're only part of the picture. Understanding what is behind your loved one's behaviors, what they mean to her, and how she experiences herself in the world can be enormously helpful to everyone involved.

If you were to ask, she'd probably tell you her food-related behaviors make sense to her and that she sees no reason to stop them. But, how can your loved one honestly believe this when what she's doing is so clearly harmful and dangerous? It's hard to imagine how anyone could truthfully defend starving or bingeing and purging. Why *does* she do this to herself?

It's not that she *wants* to be doing these things, but rather that the behaviors that go along *with* the eating disorder are incredibly helpful to her. Over time, as the illness becomes increasingly entrenched in her life, she comes to believe its presence is essential and that, in fact, she would be lost without it.

*I'm nothing without my eating disorder. I don't exist.*

*I don't know what I'd do without it.*

*I'm sure I'd die if I couldn't have it.*

## The Paradox: Dying to Live

Obviously, a paradox is at work here and it is this: Rather than random food-related thoughts and behaviors, or simply attempts to be "attractive" or "thin," the symptoms of anorexia, bulimia, and other eating disorders are powerful coping mechanisms that help an individual manage the parts of life that feel too much to bear.

In other words, even though she is participating in self-destructive eating behaviors, your loved one isn't trying to destroy herself at all; she's actually trying to *save* herself. She experiences her eating disorder as a source of support even though its symptoms are, in reality, harmful to her. Your loved one doesn't feel threatened by it. To the contrary, she feels threatened *without* it.

Ultimately, she develops an indispensable relationship with her behaviors, a relationship she relies on to help her navigate her world. It's as if your loved one has discovered a new "best friend." But this is not just any friend, this is a very powerful one who shields her from the frightening parts of life she's certain she can't handle alone.

Understanding this paradox will help you appreciate why your loved one doesn't view her eating disorder as destructive and dangerous. It also helps explain why she is so attached to the behaviors and has such a difficult time giving them up.

## How She Experiences the World

We've all had moments when we think we just can't "handle it" or "manage one more thing." Most of us experience this only on occasion, *but your loved one feels this way almost all the time.* Life is extremely intense to her, and she isn't at all sure she can deal with it. This is why she is driven to depend on anorexia or bulimia.

Strangely enough, she does find certain facets of life quite manageable. You may have noticed that she does very well academically, excels at athletics, or is a leader in student government. She may be a talented musician or writer. These elements of living don't seem to bother her at all. In fact, she may genuinely enjoy them.

At the same time, though, she experiences an underlying anxiety and fear, especially with regard to three particular aspects of life: her emotions, her beliefs about herself, and her relationships with other people. In this chapter we discuss each of these areas in detail.

## Emotions

As human beings we feel a wide range of emotions on a daily basis, such as joy, sadness, love, pain, excitement, and fear. These sensations are a normal part of everyday life. One aspect of the maturation process is developing the strength and capability to feel and embrace our emotions. For a variety of reasons, someone with an eating disorder lacks confidence in her ability to do this. Consequently, she becomes frightened of what she feels and tries to protect herself by avoiding emotions at all costs.

> *When I start to feel any emotion, I just feel as though it will sweep me away like a tidal wave. It feels so powerful that I'm afraid it will hurt me, or might even kill me. I can't stand to let my feelings happen for very long before I have to do something to make them go away.*

> *I guess I avoid emotions. I just feel they aren't okay. They're not okay to share with anyone, even my parents.*

*I'd rather die than feel.*

It might seem bizarre that bingeing, purging, starving, or over-exercising could affect what someone is feeling. However, these behaviors are very effective at reducing or covering up emotions, especially unpleasant ones like anger, disappointment, jealousy, or loneliness. The cycle of overeating and purging can provide someone with bulimia a way to both stuff down and release feelings. For someone with anorexia, the combination of not eating and excessive exercise offers a sense of control and emotional numbness.

> *I have a lot of hate and anger. I've always believed it's wrong to feel hate and anger. I've always wanted them out, out of my body, and I couldn't. I just can't get past the hate.*

> *I feel so much loneliness and guilt. I put up a pretty good shield. I don't like to get emotional, so I try not to feel. I just ignore those emotions. I pretend they don't exist. I don't like feeling that way, so I don't.*

## "I Feel Fat"

One phrase that is often repeated by many individuals with eating disorders is "I feel fat." The choice of words here is interesting to note because "fat" is not a feeling. Rather it is code for a host of feelings that are unacceptable or uncomfortable for your loved one to allow herself to experience or express.

Thus, when she says she feels fat, what she is really saying is that she feels *something else* that she doesn't know how to say in words. Because fat is considered bad in our society, what she might be saying is, "I'm a bad person" or "I hate my body" or "I am angry." Her "fat" code distills any and all complex emotional states she may encounter into one clear, simple manageable idea: *I feel fat.* This statement then becomes a mantra that can be used in any situation: to justify decisions, to avoid taking action, or, most importantly, to circumvent feelings. Her recovery will entail learning to decipher the underlying messages of this "language of fat," as well as learning to express a whole new vocabulary of honest feelings.

# Her Self-Concept

*Self-concept* or *self-image* refers to how we see ourselves, physically, psychologically, emotionally, and spiritually. For those of us who don't suffer from an eating disorder, how we feel about ourselves remains relatively constant throughout our lives. Whether we have a good or bad day and no matter how we react to it, we generally have the insight that we are always the same person. We know our likes and dislikes, our talents and shortcomings, our strengths and limitations. Having this firm, inner foundation gives us a sense of stability. Most of us take this for granted and don't usually think about how reassuring it is to always know who we are.

Regrettably, someone with an eating disorder tends to view herself negatively in many ways. If asked, she might say she's not smart enough, not thin enough, not pretty enough, not nice enough—basically that she's not good enough. Trying to discuss her erroneous self-image can be frustrating indeed. Even if you point out that she excels in her studies or athletics, is a good friend or a strong leader, she will remain steadfast in her conviction that she "can't do anything right" or "isn't good enough."

*I think I was born with a broken brain. I never felt I was good at anything. Everyone else in my family was good at something except me.*

*I have a lot of insecurities, like not being good enough, not working hard enough, not being real enough.*

*I think bad things about myself. I have felt it was a mistake when anything good happened to me. I didn't feel as if I deserved it.*

*I've always thought I was a horrible person, that I should be punished for things because I am a bad person.*

*My mom is always trying to buy me things . . . clothes and stuff. She's always asking me what I want. Doesn't she understand I don't deserve anything? I already feel so guilty about just being alive. It makes me feel even guiltier when she wants to buy me something. Why doesn't she see I'm not good enough?*

*I'm not a good enough person. I don't always have nice thoughts and I don't work hard enough. I don't deserve to have anything.*

## Perfectionism

The primary reason she is unable to see herself the way you do is because she uses "black and white" (or *absolute* or *perfectionistic*) thinking. From her perspective there are two choices: being perfect or being nothing.

Most of us accept that perfection is an ideal, not a reality. However, your loved one doesn't consider anything acceptable unless it is perfect, including herself. The problem is, of course, nothing is ever "perfect enough," leaving her continually feeling that she has failed.

There may be times when her fear of not being perfect will get the best of her and she won't even attempt something, the thought being that "if I can't be perfect, why even bother?" This line of reasoning is how she can discount any achievements. If she doesn't feel she's the absolute best in every way at whatever she attempts, none of it matters.

*I got an A+ on a history test. But I missed one extra credit question so it seems like an F.*

*Second best doesn't count.*

*It means nothing that I'm a nationally ranked tennis player. I've lost matches before, so clearly I'm not very good.*

*I was second in my class for French. I've never been so disappointed. Everyone thought I should be so happy because it was a high A, but I was only mad at myself.*

*The only place that counts is number one. There are no medals for second. You may as well be last.*

## Feeling Like a Fraud

Since her core beliefs about herself revolve around her "innate inadequacy," she is endlessly worried people around her will inevitably discover "the truth"—that she's a horrible person and a failure. She's convinced that once she is exposed for who she "really" is, no one will love her and she'll be abandoned.

It's usually obvious to family and friends that her self-concept is erroneous. Typically, though, she is so convinced the awful things she thinks about herself are true that nothing and no one can convince her otherwise. This can be very frustrating to anyone who cares about her.

Since she's so afraid of being exposed as a fraud, your loved one might try to disguise her negative feelings about herself by pretending to be especially positive and secure.

> *I try to pretend that I'm confident, but I'm not.*

> *I'm just waiting for someone to figure out who I really am. Then it's all over.*

> *People think I'm really strong, but I'm more on the weak side.*

> *I mean, if you were to ask someone like my mom and dad or even my friends they would say there's nothing wrong with me. I mean I get good grades, I have a boyfriend, I play soccer, softball. But when it comes down to it, none of it is real. The truth is I'm fat, ugly, I have hateful, I mean, really bad thoughts about myself. If people really knew me, really knew me, they would be shocked.*

## Self-Image and Body Image

For someone with an eating disorder, body image is intimately linked with self-image. Positive thoughts about her body will lead to positive thoughts about herself. If she feels "thin" or "thinner" on a particular day, she thinks more highly of herself. Conversely, if she feels "fat," she's convinced she's a bad person.

Of course, the "thin is good" and "fat is bad" messages promoted by our culture exacerbate her already-existing low self-esteem.

*If I feel small in the morning when I get dressed, then I think I'm okay. If I look in the mirror and I'm fat, or my clothes don't fit, then I feel like I'm a horrible person, like I'm a failure.*

*Weight is really connected with how you feel about yourself. Weight goes up, you feel worse about yourself. When it comes down, you feel much better.*

*If I eat perfectly all day, then I feel like a good person. If I binge or eat bad things, then I feel terrible, like I'm weak and lazy and shouldn't even be here.*

*If I got fat, I would kill myself.*

Basing one's self-esteem on body size is a precarious way to live, indeed. What's worse, your loved one's body image can change in an instant. For example, a picture of a thin model in a magazine, or a comment someone makes about how fat they think they are, or even how her clothes fit one morning can instantly affect how she feels about herself. Living with such constant self-criticism creates enormous amounts of anxiety, which she tries to manage with the eating disorder.

*I can feel okay about myself, but if I walk into the house and my mom is cooking something, I instantly feel fatter. Then I feel like I'm a horrible person and I get really depressed and feel the urge to binge.*

*I always wanted to be stick thin. Isn't that what every girl tries to look like? I mean, it's the ultimate to look like a supermodel. That would mean that I was successful, that I achieved something.*

## Relationships

A person with an eating disorder struggles greatly with relationships. Frequently, she will find relating to others confusing, frightening, and distressing. At the same time, however, she truly values relationships and wants to have people in her life. She cares deeply about those she loves.

*I don't understand it. I'm so loving and I so want to be loved. But I'm always messing things up with people. I can't figure out what to do or say and I don't know what's right, it's so confusing, unpredictable really. I'm not good at it. I feel like giving up.*

*Relationships scare me to death. I want them, then I don't. I don't think I would know what to do if I had one. I mean, I just don't like people to be close to me.*

*People thought I was really weird and I just pretended that I didn't notice, that I didn't care. But I did notice, and it hurt.*

*I always felt rejected. I didn't view myself as normal, and so I just always felt apart. I had girlfriends but nobody that was a best bud or anything. I have never had anybody that I could completely share and be intimate with. I don't think my parents thought of me as a person. I think I was like a piece of jewelry, like an ornament or something. I was something they were supposed to have, like a station wagon. In our family we never touched. I felt ignored, like I wasn't there, even though I was.*

Not surprisingly, because of her convoluted thinking, she might believe being thin enough will guarantee that people will love her.

*When I am thin my mom is so proud of me. She tells people I look great and I'm doing well. I know it's because I'm losing weight.*

*When I lost weight, everyone started praising me. I was so pleased and proud. I thought I had found the key to my happiness.*

*In the seventh grade, I got the flu and lost a lot of weight. When I went back to school, one of the popular girls asked if I lost some weight. At that moment I realized losing weight equaled being accepted. When I lost weight, I felt more confident and I started making more friends, including boys.*

At times, relationships can be demanding for anyone. Ideally, in spite of their inherent complexities and the effort required to develop and maintain them, they comfort and fulfill us.

Someone with an eating disorder wishes this was true for her, too, but her constant fear of what might happen next and her doubt that she is worthy of love make it virtually impossible for her to feel safe or secure in any relationship. So she avoids them, preferring to remain isolated. Try not to take this personally. It isn't a reflection of how much you love her or how much she loves you. It's a reflection of her profound insecurities.

## The "Salesman"

Your loved one sees danger in many places. Life is neither fun nor safe, and her fears can be paralyzing. She is afraid of losing control of her emotions and of getting hurt in relationships. She is afraid and exhausted by her own thoughts. Something has to happen. . . and then it does. She discovers the safety and predictability of a relationship with food.

To conceptualize this process and why your loved one doesn't resist its onset, we find it helpful to imagine the eating disorder as a "salesman." Although having an eating disorder is a personal and internal experience, visualizing it as separate entity can be useful for the purposes of clarity and understanding.

Imagine this salesman recognizes that your loved one is in desperate need of a way to cope with her life. This particular type of salesman happens to have a "product" that bolsters feelings of confidence, power, and invulnerability. He knows he has just what she's looking for and offers her a deal she can't resist.

In return for minor changes in her behavior, such as eating less fat or no sugar, or exercising an hour every day, he'll help her feel terrific. She doesn't think he's asking too much of her, so she unwittingly accepts.

In the early stages of the agreement, you might not notice any changes; it may appear that your loved one is just trying to eat in a healthy way or lose a little weight. In fact, at this point, she herself might not feel different, believing she's only making minor adjustments to her lifestyle.

Soon, though, the salesman returns to demand more: If she wants to continue to receive the benefits he offers she must make increasingly dramatic changes to her food and/or exercise behaviors. And each time he returns, she agrees to whatever he commands her to do. The result is that the eating disorder becomes more and more entrenched in her life and begins to exact a greater and greater toll. Over time, her dependence upon the food and exercise-related behaviors escalates to a point where she becomes exceedingly resistant to letting them go, largely because she believes she *can't* without suffering dire consequences.

> *It's the only thing I can trust. It helps me deal with all my shit. It has never let me down, it has never lied to me. I mean, what else could you ask for?*

Although it's tempting to view him as such, the salesman isn't a horrible, reprehensible creature. He is a sincere believer in the product he offers. And in fact, in his own way, he is assisting your loved one by helping her cope with her fears, insecurities, and lack of self-confidence. For this reason, while it's easy to vilify her eating disorder, it's important not to do so. The relationship between your loved one and her illness is complicated. She really does experience it as a friend. Her main focus is on how much it helps her and how consistent and reliable it is.

> *It will never let me down. It's always there for me.*

> *It won't ever surprise me.*

> *I know how it behaves, and what it wants from me. It has rules and as long as I follow the rules, I get the benefits.*

> *I do what it says. And it does what it promises.*

## Increasing Dependence and Isolation

Not surprisingly, your loved one's relationship with the anorexia or bulimia (the salesman) takes a lot of time and energy. As she relies more and more on that relationship to feel good, she will begin to withdraw from her relationships with other people. She may still participate in some activities, but her friendships and connections to family members will become increasingly superficial. Eventually, she will no longer have the time, energy, or even the desire to be with people or to be social in any way, spending the majority of her time alone.

This is how the eating disorder turns into her primary, if not sole, relationship. Again, try not to take this personally. It has nothing to do with how much she cares about you. She's not withdrawing because she's annoyed with you or doesn't love you. It's that the eating disorder demands her complete attention and "loyalty." For this reason, a key component of recovery is to carefully examine the relationship with "the salesman," which ultimately will result in strengthening her connections with other people and with her healthy self.

**PART II**

{ *Hearing Their Words* }

# CHAPTER 4

# Understanding Anorexia

## *In Their Own Words*

An individual with anorexia develops a belief that if she could just look and feel thin enough, her life would improve dramatically. Doing whatever is required to lose weight and realize this sense of thinness becomes her fundamental goal.

Unfortunately, this strategy is intrinsically problematic because someone with anorexia rarely reaches a weight or body size she deems thin enough. Even if an "acceptable" level of thinness is achieved, any contentment is short lived. Soon thereafter, feelings of distress about herself and her life return, and with them the renewed conviction that if she can lose just a bit *more* weight, the suffering will disappear forever.

*Over the years my goal—what I wanted to weigh—has gotten lower. I keep thinking that someday I will feel good about my body and I will be, you know, happy. Maybe not hysterically happy, but I will feel good about my life. I don't ever feel good, like I think you're supposed to feel. . . . When I do lose some weight, any weight, I feel better. Not great, but better.*

*I have a weight, a weight that I want to get to. I know I'll feel better when I get there.*

*Once I started losing weight, then the more weight I lost, the more terrified I was of gaining anything back. I felt like everything I was getting out of it would be taken away.*

*I lost weight, I know that, but I still have a ways to go. . . . It hasn't led to me feeling better.*

*My goal weight gets lower and lower.*

*I don't know what it's about, but I have a weight I want to be at and I know things will be better, I will feel better about myself.*

## Doesn't She See What She's Doing?

How someone can lose so much weight and become dangerously thin without realizing it is a mystifying aspect of anorexia. We have often heard family members say, "She *must* see she's too small, how could she not?" or "Why doesn't she just eat?" But, your loved one is neither lying, nor being contrary or rebellious. When she looks at herself in the mirror, reads a number on the scale, or puts on clothes, she truly believes her body is too big and, what's more, it's all her fault.

## How Is She Judging What's Thin?

If an individual cannot see herself accurately with regard to her weight and size, and if actual numbers do not convince her of what she is doing to her body, how does she measure her "thinness"?

For someone with anorexia, thinness is measured by how she *feels*: she believes she is thin only if she *feels* thin. What a scale might read, what you or anyone else might tell her, is irrelevant. She simply will not believe anything other than her own perceptions.

> I know I'm just huge. Completely huge. My parents and my doctor say I'm too thin; that I could die. But they don't see the truth. I know I'm fat because I can feel it.

> It doesn't matter what the scale says. Scales lie. What I feel is a better measure of if I'm fat. I don't lie.

> Why don't people tell me the truth about what I weigh? I think they just want me to be fatter. Or they want me to feel like I'm a better person by not thinking I'm so fat. Don't they understand that I know how big I am? I can tell by how my body feels.

The fact that she feels fat and denies being thin is based on inner experiences, not objective measurements. As strange as this may seem, it is her reality and demonstrates why anorexia (along with other eating disorders) actually has very little to do with food or weight. When she tells you, "I feel fat," she believes she's declaring a truth about her physical self—that she *is* fat.

In reality, her experience has little to do with the actual size of her body at the moment. Without realizing it, what she's really doing is communicating something about her emotional state. The fact that someone uses food, weight, or her body to convey her emotions is central to why someone develops an eating disorder, and it is discussed throughout this book.

## Does She Feel Her Whole Body Is Too Big?

Some people with anorexia see their entire bodies as too large, whereas others are dissatisfied with specific parts or areas.

*I have fat everywhere, especially on my back and stomach.*

*I have never looked in the mirror and seen what anyone else sees. I have never seen a thin person.*

*I liked that I could feel certain bones sticking out and I liked that when I took a bath it hurt because I was so thin. . . I always felt like I could lose more weight. I always think my hips are too big.*

*I look down at me right now and I am huge. I hesitate to take off my shirt because I know I am wearing a tank top and have the flabbiest arms.*

## Why Does She Want to be Thin?

The false impression that thinness in and of itself will make a difference in your loved one's life is what motivates her to go to extremes to achieve what she thinks is an "ideal" weight. But there is much more involved than just a thin body. Anorexic behaviors, such as restricting eating, counting calories or fat grams, or planning her daily food intake, produce specific physical and emotional states that help her avoid aspects of her life she feels are unmanageable. Let's explore five of the most common ways anorexia might help someone cope.

## "It makes me feel better"

Seriously restricting food intake has dramatic consequences for any of us. It makes us feel physically weak and fatigued, and negatively affects concentration, memory, and thought processes. One of the fascinating effects of too little nutrition is emotional "numbness." People also describe this sensation as feeling "out of touch," "in a different zone," or "dead."

This numbness is crucial to the person with anorexia who often feels overwhelmed by difficult emotions and tries desperately to avoid them. Once the disturbing emotions are dulled, she feels safer, less vulnerable, and calmer, as if she has things under control. As long as your loved one continues to limit her food intake, she can maintain this false sense of security—at least for a while.

> When I don't eat I feel flatlined. It's like I'm made of rubber or something. I have no emotions.

> It's kind of addictive feeling in that "zone" I get into when I don't eat, or don't eat enough. . . . I miss that place when I am not there.

> It has always been easier for me to deal with physical pain, so if I feel some pain because I'm not eating, that's okay with me.

> When I am really into it, I don't feel a lot . . . I don't feel, physically or emotionally.

## "My life is simpler"

Restricting food intake also reduces her life to only a few thoughts. *"What did I eat today?" "Do my clothes feel tighter than yesterday?" "How many calories did my lunch have?" "How long did I exercise this morning?"* By focusing on weight and food-related matters, she avoids dealing with life and all its complexities, uncertainties, and choices. She is left with an impression she very much desires: her life is stable and predictable, simple and clear-cut.

> If I don't eat, then it is a good day. But if I give in and eat, then the whole day is ruined.

> I didn't have time to think about anything else because I was too busy counting calories or planning my next workout.

> It's not that I was avoiding life. Anorexia was my life!

## "I feel powerful"

Because an anorexic individual has the discipline to restrict the calories she ingests and ignore her body's hunger signals, she sees herself as powerful.

She feels "in control" of herself, her body, and consequently her life. She may even feel that if she "succumbs" to eating, she is "weak" and this will make her all the more determined to succeed at self-starvation.

*If I don't eat, I feel really powerful, like nothing can harm me. But if I eat anything, even a piece of fruit, everything comes crashing down around me and is ruined. I feel weak and like I can't do anything.*

*When I'm not eating, I feel I am in control. When I do eat, I feel I lose that control and I want to get it back.*

*When I do eat, I feel like a failure. It's the worst feeling in the world to have food in my stomach.*

*It was clearly a way for me to feel some control in my life. It was something that my parents couldn't control.*

*If I don't eat, I feel like I'm happier. I just feel stronger and better. I feel proud, like I can do that. I can control that. I feel strong.*

## "I Need to Feel Special"

Although someone with anorexia may be talented, accomplished, and unique, she rarely sees herself that way. She more likely thinks of herself as stupid, uninspiring, or incompetent. Despite any evidence you present to illustrate her wonderful qualities, she can't believe it's true.

Severely limiting what we eat is difficult to do and requires a great deal of commitment and effort. Consequently, the ability to do it so successfully can make your loved one feel that this is the one special talent or skill that sets her apart from others, and she will cling to it.

*The more I could stand the hunger and everything that went with it, the stronger I felt. I knew not everyone could do this, that it was hard work, and I was proud I was brave enough and strong enough.*

*Starving was the only thing I ever did that showed I was different than other people. Not just different, better.*

*I don't know why nothing I did felt good enough. I got good grades, I had friends, people said they liked me. I don't know. Restricting seemed good enough.*

It's important to understand that no one consciously chooses to have anorexia or any other eating disorder. Although her behaviors may look as if she is being manipulative, "bratty," or simply trying to get attention, these disorders are extremely complex. The mere fact that self-imposed starvation gives an individual a feeling of uniqueness, not her personality or innate talents, only serves to underline the distorted and inaccurate view she has of herself.

*I figured if I couldn't be the prettiest, then I would be the thinnest. Something to make me unique or special.*

*It's real clear for me; I want to be thin because that's what other people want, and it matters to me what other people think of me. I want them to think I'm worth knowing.*

*I never felt good about myself or like there was anything special about me. When I first lost weight, people noticed, and so then I thought that was something people would notice about me. I would get attention for it, not only from my family, but from everyone. It was a way for me to be special.*

## "Relationships Are Less Scary"

Earlier we discussed the anxiety someone with an eating disorder experiences in relationships. She usually feels insecure, as if she has to "earn" love, and then be careful not to "do anything wrong" that may cause the other person to leave. Such beliefs lead to chronic feelings of uncertainty and instability.

Anorexia helps her avoid these feelings because it mutes emotional experience. Consequently, your loved one may not be subjected to the same level of anxiety and vulnerability she would normally feel in relationships, making her less timid. She also believes pursuing thinness is something people will be pleased about and admire her for.

This belief is often reinforced at the onset of anorexia, particularly if people say positive and approving things about the way her body is changing. Her assumption is she has found the key to making herself loveable and valuable, and this makes her feel more confident. As a side effect, she becomes convinced that if she ever deviates from thinness in any way, she will suddenly become unlovable and abandoned.

> *Some people play guitar, some dance, some do whatever. I starve. It's less common. Anyone can do those other things. I know, I did them.*

> *People like thin people. Guys like thin girls. Girls envy other girls who are thin. As long as I am thin, I will have something.*

> *Not eating is hard. What do people think? That I'm having a great time doing this? No way. I work at it. If it was easy, everyone would do it. Only people who are very strong can pull it off.*

> *Being thin or having a nice body will get you a lot. People like thin. I knew I had the boyfriends I had in part because of what I looked like . . . the fact that I was thin.*

> *My mom started noticing how I looked. She seemed pleased...like suddenly I was worth taking shopping or hanging around with. I guess she was embarrassed by me before.*

> *My family, they only like me if I'm not eating. They praise me and think I'm cool. But if I gain weight or eat too much they criticize me. They only love me if I'm thin.*

The anxiety, confusion, and discomfort related to having relationships can also prompt her to avoid them, even though doing so makes her sad and lonely.

*I used to like being around people. I mean, in high school I was always out doing stuff with my friends. Now they don't call anymore because I've been avoiding them. . . . I think that's just as well. . . . The eating disorder takes a lot of my time.*

*I really don't need anyone right now in my life.*

*I think relationships cause me more grief than it's worth.*

## Isn't Food Just Food?

For most people, food is a simple thing. An apple is just an apple—a food we may like, dislike, or don't particularly care about one way or another. It does not generally frighten us or hold any moral value.

For someone who has anorexia, though, an apple has meaning far beyond being just a piece of fruit. Such a person will judge every bite that she puts into her mouth. Some foods are regarded as "good" or "safe" and others as "bad," "off limits," or "evil." She fears such foods will harm her by making her fat, which means she is also "bad," "lazy," or "worthless" for eating them. Her relationship with food is a source of conflict and anguish, and unfortunately one that becomes increasingly agonizing as the disorder progresses.

*I wish I could take food at face value. . . . I'm so afraid of it. Even something like a grape seems so dangerous to me. . . . Like it will damage me in some way if I eat it.*

*I just don't get it...how can someone even think of eating a piece of pizza? I can't even imagine putting that grease and fat into my mouth. I'd never do that in a million years. I'd rather die.*

*When I first started with my eating disorder most things were still okay. . . . Then certain meats became bad, then all meat, then milk stuff . . . then even fruits became off limits. And after awhile, I was afraid to put anything into my mouth. Once something becomes a bad food, then it is always off limits.*

*I can't make it okay again.*

*When I was a kid, I could eat anything I wanted and not even think about it. Foods weren't good or bad. I don't know what changed. I don't get it. I know intellectually that a food shouldn't be bad or good, but I don't feel that way at all.*

*My mom makes this casserole that has cheese on top of it. She doesn't understand why I can't have any. I don't understand how she can think that cheese is safe to eat; it is such a bad food.*

## Does She Have Anorexia If She Binges and Purges?

People diagnosed with anorexia sometimes engage in behaviors usually associated with other types of eating disorders. For example, your loved one may occasionally binge, or binge and purge. She may even think she does *not* have anorexia precisely because she engages in these other behaviors. While bingeing and purging is the primary way of dealing with food for someone with bulimia, and bingeing without purging is the main characteristic of binge-eating disorder, occasional practice of either of these behaviors is not uncommon for someone with anorexia.

*If I think I've eaten more than 500 calories in a day, I will purge everything else I might eat. It seems that anytime I put anything in my mouth I think that I ate too much. My limit seems to be two bites.*

*If I eat anything other than my veggies, I usually will throw it up.*

*It's like, for me, it could be anything. I mean, it's more like a feeling. A feeling that I ate too much. I don't have to eat a lot. I mean, I could be having my cabbage soup and think I should purge.*

*It depends on how I'm feeling that day, what kind of day I'm having. Sometimes I can eat some things, then other times I have to throw up when all I have is a glass of water.*

*It could be anything, a bagel or a muffin. It's not what you think a binge should be.*

# Jacquie's Story

To put all this in context, we offer the story of Jacquie, a young woman who developed anorexia. Jacquie is as unique as any of us and, consequently, so is her story. At the same time, her experiences parallel those of others with this disorder, and are therefore useful in illustrating how and why anorexia develops. In her story, you may recognize your own and find new understanding and support.

## Jacquie

Jacquie began treatment as an 18-year-old high school graduate. At the time she had plans to attend college to pursue a degree in history, with a long-term goal of becoming a high school teacher.

Jacquie's parents divorced when she was seven years old. Her father moved into a nearby apartment and initially remained a big part of her life. However, as time passed, she saw him less and less often because his job required him to be out of town for several weeks at a time. Her parents' divorce impacted Jacquie greatly. She missed her father and longed to have her parents back together. When her father remarried and moved to another town, she would visit only once a month, and felt like an "outsider" or "guest," not a member of the extended family. Her mother neither remarried nor dated after the divorce, and because Jacquie had no siblings, life at home was lonely.

When she was ten, Jacquie discovered and immediately fell in love with dancing and was soon taking classes three to four times a week. Dance gave her a way to "escape life." When she danced, nothing else mattered, and her abilities improved rapidly. The instructors at the dance studio frequently acknowledged Jacquie's natural talents and she won several competitions. She dreamed of eventually pursuing a career as a professional dancer and touring all over the world.

Dance had the added benefit of bringing mother and daughter closer together, which Jacquie cherished. The two of them spent lots of time talking in the car, driving back and forth from classes and performances.

One day when she was in her early teenage years, a teacher commented that Jacquie looked as if she had gained some weight. The instructor went on to say she hoped Jacquie would not develop large breasts because that would interfere with her ability to continue dancing at a competitive level. To make matters worse, that same week Jacquie overheard an aunt tell her mother she thought Jacquie was getting big and better watch out because "boys don't like heavy girls."

Determined not to let anything interfere with her chances to dance or date, Jacquie resolved to eat less. She began to severely restrict her food intake until it amounted to less than 1000 calories per day, but continued to dance as much as she always had. At first, she felt ravenous and constantly thought about food. Nevertheless, she maintained her self-imposed calorie limit and only ate foods low in fat. She often managed her intense desire for food by buying something she craved, taking a bite to get a taste, then spiting it out so the calories wouldn't be ingested. Eventually, as the eating disorder progressed, both her cravings and need for food lessened.

As Jacquie's weight began to drop, her dance instructors told her she looked better and her skills improved. In addition, classmates admired her ability to be so disciplined about what and when she ate. "I was totally consumed by it at this point. All the positive attention. I felt I was really on the right track."

It wasn't long before Jacquie's mother became worried about her daughter's dramatic weight loss and fixation on food. When she approached her with these concerns, Jacquie responded with intense anger and told her mother not to interfere in her life. Her mother spoke with the mothers of other dancers and typically received the response that Jacquie had a "dancer's body" and not to worry.

It wasn't until Jacquie fainted one day during rehearsal that people recognized her frail physical condition. The dance company demanded Jacquie take a leave of absence to avoid risking her health. Not surprisingly, this was extremely discouraging for Jacquie. Even so, she could not bring herself to eat enough to resume dancing.

Ironically, the longer she was away from dance the greater were her fears of gaining weight and feelings of being out of control. Also, because she was not using up as many calories, Jacquie began to exercise to compensate. Her regimen included running three to four miles every day and riding her bike several times a week. She added aerobics on days she felt "extra fat."

## The Reasons for Jacquie's Anorexia

Dance gave Jacquie a sense of belonging and purpose. "Some people identify themselves as human beings, or as accountants, or doctors, or whatever. I was a dancer. It was the only way I knew myself." Dancing also relieved day-to-day pressures and drowned out feelings about her parents' divorce and her father's diminishing role.

What's more, throughout her young life, Jacquie struggled with self-confidence and often felt she lacked things others possessed. She never felt as if she was as smart or pretty as others. But when she danced, she felt good about herself.

> *"It was like, since I could do this dance thing, it made up for everything else that was wrong with me. On some days I even thought I was better than everyone else. I mean, like I was a better person somehow. I know it sounds ridiculous, but that's how it felt. And it felt good, for once in my life."*

Jacquie thought dancing was a guaranteed part of her life until she heard the teacher's comment regarding her figure.

> *"I understood what she said to mean I was going to lose dance. And that there was nothing I could do about it. But maybe there was something I could do, if I figured out how to stop my body from developing. I had never thought of that possibility before, that I'd lose dance. It really hadn't ever entered my mind. Ever."*

Jacquie's interpretation of this authority figure's remark left her believing her fate was suddenly not in her own hands. Desperate to regain a sense of control, she shifted her focus to regulating food and weight. The objective was twofold: thwart further development of her body and provide herself with a sense of predictability and stability.

Unfortunately, this new attempt to feel invulnerable and in control turned out to be far from perfect. Jacquie rarely felt thin enough, regardless of how much she weighed. Any moment of satisfaction with her appearance was short-lived. Regrettably, she did not know any other way to cope with life. Anorexia was now firmly embedded in her identity.

Entering treatment was Jacquie's attempt to "find out if there was another way of being." She missed the days when she felt free and happy. Although she didn't know exactly what recovery might entail and was frightened by the idea of talking to people about her eating disorder, she was willing to try.

# CHAPTER 5

# Understanding Bulimia

## *In Their Own Words*

As described in the previous chapter, the fundamental belief of an individual with anorexia is that being thin will make her life better, which causes her to develop a negative relationship with food that is, for the most part, consistent, straightforward, and clear: food is bad.

Someone with bulimia also has a difficult relationship with food, but it is one that is both complex and ambivalent. Food is seen as an escape *and* a threat. These conflicting viewpoints account for the cycle of bingeing then purging. As the term implies, the binge/purge cycle is made up of two distinct but related phases: the binge and the purge. We'll examine each in detail in this chapter, but generally speaking, bingeing refers to a discrete period of time when an individual ingests a certain amount of food, and purging refers to the use of some method to rid one's body of that food.

Bingeing tends to provide your loved one with a sense of comfort and security by producing a "numb" or "calm" state. Shortly after bingeing, though, she becomes horrified by what she's ingested and turns to purging to empty herself of the food. Purging serves a threefold function: eliminating what she's just eaten, extending her feeling of emotional deadness, and restoring a sense of control or order.

> I'll be so anxious, all I can think of that might help is eating and eating. For a few minutes it does help, and I feel better. Then it all starts to crash in on me again . . . all the anxiety and dread. But it's worse then because I also feel guilty about having eaten all that. So I'm really screwed at this point. But then I start to purge, and that makes me feel calmer again for a while.

The cycle of eating, panicking, and purging can be confusing and unsettling, often leaving her feeling "crazy" or "messed up" inside. She doesn't understand why she's acting like this and can't figure out how to stop her destructive behavior.

> I must be insane. Why would anyone do this to herself? Every day I tell myself, "Okay, I just won't start eating and everything will be okay." But for some reason I have to start to binge, I can't help myself. And then what am I supposed to do, just leave the food in my stomach? No way. So I go throw up. But the whole time I'm telling myself, "You are one messed up girl."

> It feels so crazy. I can't stop myself. Once I've started to binge, there's no going back. Usually in my life I have such strong willpower, but when it comes to eating, I'm so weak. I don't get it. It's frustrating.

> I wake up each morning and I know it will happen. And I hate it. I mean, I hate the out-of-control parts of it. I like the eating part. It's great to be able to eat whatever I want and not gain weight, but I hate how chaotic it feels, like I'm some wild animal on a rampage. I can't believe I behave like that. I'm always so shy and quiet. People would never believe I do this.

# The Binge

Though a variety of circumstances can lead someone to binge, commonly the person feels highly distressed, threatened, and anxious. The source of these feelings vary, and may include a problem in a relationship, feelings of anger, negative thoughts about who she is as a person, or even physical discomfort. When these feelings seem too overwhelming and intense for her to bear, she turns to bingeing as a way to cope.

Once she begins to eat, everything seems to stand still. Her exclusive focus becomes getting the food down. Whatever she'd previously been feeling is no longer in her awareness, and this emotionally "numb" state is not only tolerable, but vastly preferable.

*When I'm bingeing, I'm not recognizing what I'm feeling.*

*It's like I'm not conscious during the binge. It's not until after I have eaten I realize I shouldn't have done that.*

*I always feel possessed when I am bingeing.*

*I never remember a binge afterwards . . . It's like I am checked out during binges.*

*It's a numb feeling. The only thing I can compare it to is having a buzz. I am not connected to anything in reality. I am just kind of numb and sitting back and observing everything. Like even observing myself.*

*I watch TV when I binge. I watch movies. I close the door, lock it, put down the blinds, turn on the TV, and it is just like a total escape. It's like my mind is free. I am totally in a world of my own. It is like I am happy, comfortable. I am content.*

*I sometimes get excited about bingeing because I know I am going to get an adrenaline rush. The feeling that I get during a binge is like taking a drug. It is very soothing, very nurturing, and it feels good.*

## What Kinds of Emotions Lead Her to Binge?

Typically, bingeing provides a person with a way to eliminate emotions *she* considers too negative or difficult to handle, such as anxiety, anger, and fear. But sometimes even positive feelings, such as joy or enthusiasm, feel too intense and must be moderated.

> Emotions feel so bright, like going outside without sunglasses in the blazing sun. You feel like you have to shield your eyes. I feel like I have to shield myself from feelings. It's like they might burn me if I don't.

> If my heart hurts, I will go binge.

> I'll binge over anything. Really...if I'm happy, sad, hyper, it doesn't matter. Any emotions feel too much for me. They are all so extreme. I don't like any of them.

> Feelings scare me. I don't care if they are good feelings or bad feelings. They are all scary.

> I don't go to my dad's house much because when I am there I eat and throw up. I feel very uncomfortable there. I can't be myself. I don't feel I'm accepted by him.

> Before this last binge, I was feeling really depressed and out of control about a conversation I had with my mother. . . There are certain reasons why I binge. It's like when I am tired, when I am angry, and when I am lonely. These are the emotions I have to watch out for.

## What Is Emotional Hunger?

Physical hunger occurs when our body is in need of food. Emotional hunger is related to psychological or emotional needs, such as closeness, connection, safety, or constancy. When we are satisfied emotionally, we feel calm and settled, as if we are "full." When these needs are not met, we feel a void or a hole inside that is experienced as an inner "hunger."

Individuals with bulimia try to fill this hole by eating. No matter how much is consumed, though, the emptiness remains because *emotional needs can never be satisfied with food.*

*I use food for comfort. I don't use food for energy... I look at people who eat well or who eat because they are hungry and I am so envious.*

*I have a hole in my heart. It's a hole because my heart broke a few years ago, and nothing I do can ever fill it up.*

*I am hungry, and just not physically but emotionally, in a way, I think. By the end of the day, I have just felt so much shit I just feel worn down, and I eat to mellow out a little bit... It feels good. The bingeing feels good, eating feels good. It makes me feel good.*

*Food fills me up on a feeling level.*

*For me, food means security. Like if I knew there was food there whenever I wanted it, I feel security around that. I guess it is comforting... in a way, it's real controllable.*

*I'm so sad. Just sad and sad and sad. Day after day. And I keep hoping that if I keep eating, the sadness will go away.*

## What Constitutes a Binge?

Sometimes an individual will binge on whatever she can get her hands on at the moment. Most of the time, her choices are deliberate and, for some people, meticulously planned. A binge is typically comprised of foods she usually denies herself because she considers them "bad" or "unsafe." While one person might prefer dessert-like foods that are high in fat and/or sugar, another might crave entrées, such as steak and potatoes or macaroni and cheese. Foods that are a source of comfort or those that were forbidden when she was a child are common choices.

*Someone once asked me why don't I just binge on carrots. That way I wouldn't have to worry about it. I just laughed. I can eat carrots any day... why would I waste stomach room on carrots?*

*I love hamburgers. As a kid we never got to eat them. I don't even know why. But now I binge on them...it's like I'm rebelling or something. But if I'm not bingeing I'll never touch red meat. It's so gross. I don't see how people can eat it.*

*I was in the mood for sweets. It's like sometimes I've got to have my sweets. I don't do it too often, because if I didn't get rid of it through purging I would get fat. So I went to the store and bought a half-gallon of chocolate chip ice cream and two candy bars. I went home and had two big bowls of ice cream and the candy.*

*High fat. High sugar. All the gross things I won't usually let myself have.*

*I plan my binges carefully. I think about it all day at school and plan what to buy. I only want bad stuff. As fattening as you can get. Then I go to the store and buy it all. I have to have exactly what I want or the binge doesn't feel right. It's a kind of tradition.*

What is deemed a binge is subjective. For one person, it might mean consuming an enormous amount of food at one time. For another, it's eating what is usually considered a regular-sized meal. Still another might believe *anything* she eats constitutes a binge. What makes this all the more complicated is that one's personal criteria for whether a particular event is a binge can fluctuate from day to day, or even within a particular day.

Often, what determines whether an individual is bingeing is her sense of "crossing the line," which divides what is acceptable eating behavior and what is not. Once she feels she has crossed this line, she needs to make herself purge.

Where the line is differs for every individual and is based on a variety of factors. One person's might be the moment she feels full, whereas another's is when she realizes she's consumed a certain number of calories or a particular food she considers "bad." She may sometimes know exactly where she is in relation to the line and other times be surprised when she finds herself crossing it suddenly. Once the line has been crossed, though, there's no turning back, and refraining from continuing the binge and eventually purging is rare.

> I don't know where it is until I get there. That point. But I always know the second I've hit it. Something tells me, you are so fat, you have to go purge.

> If I've decided I'm going to go all day without eating, then I eat something... anything, even two calories, that's a binge.

> Anything for me can be a binge... It's just when I think I've eaten too much... That could be a muffin or bagel or a full meal.

> I can go to a dinner party and I will have something that is really minimal. If I eat a little bit too much, then I will indulge in everything, and I will eat like there is no tomorrow.

> Once I've gone over it, that imaginary line, there's no turning back. You'd have to tie me to a tree to get me to not purge. I'd still probably find a way, even tied to the tree. People don't get it, I can't stop it.

> It's like I am eating and I take the next bite and I have gone over the edge... and I can't stop.

## The Purge

During the binge, your loved one is distracted, soothed, and calmed. At first, all seems well. But a problem looms. Once the binge is over, the very feelings and thoughts she was trying to avoid return, and with them comes the need to do something to relieve her overwhelmed state. Moreover, she now has the additional anxiety of having consumed an amount of food she finds unacceptable, adding guilt to her list of already overpowering emotions. She turns to purging as a solution.

*I always think bingeing is going to solve it all, whatever bad things I'm feeling. It does, for a few minutes. But it never lasts, and then I have to find something else to make myself feel better.*

*Why can't it last? I feel so good during a binge.*

*I hate to see it... my stomach sticks out. It's rounded, not flat. I can't stand it. I have to fix it.*

*My mood gets worse after I binge. I feel really disgusted with myself for bingeing. . . It's not normal.*

*During the binge, I feel really good. Then I realize I ate this whole thing and then there is the shame and anger. I realize that I lost control. It is kind of a sinful gluttony.*

*I just can't believe it after I binge. I can't believe I'd do something like that. I usually want to kill myself because I feel so desperate and depressed.*

*I'd rather die than have to live with having binged and not be able to do anything about it.*

## What, Exactly, Is Purging?

Although the most common method of purging is self-induced vomiting, other methods exist, such as the abuse of laxatives or diuretics and excessive exercise. Her primary technique may change over time, or she might use a variety of methods depending on the circumstances.

*The only thing I can think of is to make myself throw up. I know it's gross, but after bingeing I feel so fat and disgusting. I have to do something about it right away.*

*After I eat I go to the gym and get on one of the machines. Once I'm on it, I get into some kind of a trance, where everything feels calmer, more settled. Nothing else gives me that feeling. I can lose hours being in that trance.*

*Throwing up is my usual method of getting rid of the food. I don't trust anything else. I wouldn't know how long I had to exercise to be sure I had done enough. And I can't wait long enough for laxatives or anything to take effect. I have to do something NOW!*

*I used to put my finger down my throat. I've been doing it so long that now all I have to do is lean over. I guess that should worry me, but, really, I'm only thinking I'm glad I can get rid of the food.*

*I mostly use laxatives. I've heard they only get rid of water, not what you've eaten. I don't believe it. I like them because they make me feel like I have been cleaned out, like I can start all over.*

*I make myself throw up. I do it in the shower so I can watch everything come up. I try to be as violent as possible. The meaner I can be to myself, the more I feel as if I've been punished for being so stupid. Sometimes I make my throat bleed.*

## How Does Purging Help?

Purging fulfills several needs. First and foremost, it immediately relieves the experience of physical pressure resulting from food in her stomach. As a consequence, the individual with bulimia is comforted knowing that the calories she just ingested will not cause her to gain weight.

*I felt like I got everything I wanted. I got to eat the hamburger and didn't have to suffer the consequences of gaining weight... If I kept the food in my body, I would continue to feel full and fat. I mean, I don't like that feeling.*

*During the purge, it was like the unique feeling of getting rid of a pimple. That you are getting rid of something that is going to cause harm. You are getting rid of something bad.*

*It's great because you get to enjoy eating with only a little guilt in the back of your mind because you know that you are going to throw it up. Then you throw it up and you wipe your face off and you brush your teeth and that's it. You just go on with your day. You're not hungry because you did this to your body and you get rid of the calories.*

Second, similar to bingeing, purging induces a desirable intoxicated or "out-of-it" emotional state.

*When it's time to purge, it's all I can think about. It's intoxicating. It's like I am in an alcohol-induced stupor. Everything feels numb. I remember getting into a minor accident because I was so anxious to get home to purge.*

*I've talked to people who've done crack cocaine. They say that the only time in their lives they feel good about themselves is the few moments they are high on crack. I can relate to that . . . it's like the feeling I get from purging—like a high, almost.*

*I have more confidence on the days that I purge. I feel like I am on top of the world, that I can do anything and that no one can stop me.*

*I am so out of it during a purge. I really like that feeling. It seems like nothing can touch me, or at least that I won't care if it does.*

Third, she may feel she recovers some sense of control after the "chaos" and "mess" of bingeing.

*When I purge, I get renewal. Just after I purge, it is like everything is calm and it's all started again. Everything is okay. I clean the toilet, put on my shirt, and it's like my stomach is flat again and I am in control again.*

*All I know is that I felt better after I purged. I felt less full and more in control. It was a control issue. Hey, I screwed up by eating that second hamburger but got control back by taking care of it.*

*Throwing up feels good. It's a feeling of getting rid of the food and getting back control. You couldn't control putting the food inside your body, so you barf and get rid of it. Then you have control again.*

## After the Purge

The period after the purge may bring a mix of positive and negative emotions, such as a sense of relief, or frustration and disappointment. Feeling worn out and exhausted, both physically and emotionally, is common.

*After purging, I feel like I have succeeded.*

*After I purge, I feel disappointed in myself, really sad and scared. It is like really, really scary because it is so out of control.*

*I feel good, but exhausted. I'm wiped out, physically and emotionally.*

*I get a break for a while, at least . . . Afterwards, the feelings, all the shit comes back.*

*I feel really disgusted with myself. I look down into the toilet and I think what a horrible thing I did. It's not normal, and so disgusting. . . I just feel really disgusted with myself.*

*Sometimes I'm relieved but also sad, like I wish I didn't have to do it.*

## *Why Does She Keep it Secret?*

Your loved one will usually hide her behavior from nearly everyone, especially the people she considers to be important or close. With very few exceptions, bingeing and purging takes place in settings where she is alone or where she can conceal what she is doing.

One reason she hides her behavior is the considerable shame and guilt that surrounds bingeing and purging. She views her actions as uncontrollable or a sign of weakness and presumes the judgment of others will be similar. She also may believe they could never understand or forgive her for having an eating disorder.

Like someone who has anorexia, a person with bulimia very much wants her life to look good to the outside world and to have people respect and think highly of her. She worries others won't like or love her if they find out she is hiding a terrible secret.

*I was very secretive about it, and only did it when nobody was around.*

*This is not socially acceptable. You can't say to the lady in the bathroom, "Oh, don't mind me, I'm going to go in here to throw up. I am bulimic."*

*The shame of all of this is overwhelming. I'm so weak. The deception, I think, gives me a lot of guilty feelings. I feel guilty that I'm deceiving others. Deception is wrong. It is really dishonest to deceive someone like that, especially when they are paying for the food.*

*I get out of control. I can't stop. I don't want anyone to see me that way.*

*I don't tell people about my eating disorder because I don't want them to feel sorry for me. I don't want them to think they need to look at me differently, like, "Oh, that girl has an eating disorder. We'd better not invite her out to dinner."*

*I have to be alone when I binge. I can't have anyone around me because I would be embarrassed.*

*I would wake up in the middle of the night and go eat, hoping my roommates wouldn't hear.*

*I would never binge in front of anyone. I'd feel like a pig.*

More often than not, she believes her best chance of keeping the bulimia is for it to remain hidden. Should anyone find out, they might want her to get help. Though to friends and family, pursuing treatment seems a positive step, her fear is that such a move would result in the eating disorder being "taken away" from her.

*It is real secretive, a real private thing, and that is kind of the neat part of it, because it is so private. Nobody knows. It's all mine.*

*I don't feel like I have anything in my life. I don't even feel like my life is my own. But my eating disorder is my own. I don't want anyone to take that away from me. They can do whatever else they want, but they can't have my eating disorder.*

*I know it's gross. But it is mine. No one can touch it. I can keep it forever.*

Although it is far more common to conceal one's eating behavior, in some cases an individual will intentionally leave signs of a binge or purge to be discovered by others. Generally, she does this in an attempt to communicate some kind of message that she cannot convey using words.

*I don't know why I did it, why I left little signs around that I knew my parents would find. Everything was always so neat in our house. Everything had its proper place. My telltale food tidbits were something very out of the ordinary in our house. I knew it freaked them out.*

*Making a mess is my way of showing how angry I am. I'd never be able to tell them, but if leave some food in the toilet, they get the point.*

*I guess I was crying out for help. I didn't realize it at the time. I just thought I wasn't being very careful about cleaning up after throwing up.*

## How Does She Hide Her Bingeing and Purging?

Because secrecy is usually crucial, an individual will go to great lengths and employ a variety of strategies to conceal her behavior from others.

*I go in my car when I eat. I throw up in there also. That way no one knows I'm doing it. Well, only the people I drive by while I'm bingeing, I guess, but I'll never see them again.*

*I'll go buy binge food from the next town over. Everyone in my town knows me now. It is so humiliating. After awhile I'll have to start driving to an even farther-away town. It gets tiring.*

*I was real sneaky about hiding my binges. I would cook one tray of brownies for my family and one for myself. That way no one pays attention to how much I eat. They don't know about the other tray.*

*We were having plumbing problems, so it wasn't a good idea for me to throw up in the toilet. So I started using three-pound coffee cans that I would fill up with vomit and keep in garbage bags, which were kept in the basement until they had to be carried up the stairs and out to the road.*

*When my roommates were home, I'd throw up in the shower, because the running water would mask the noise.*

*I make the rounds at fast food restaurants. I try to vary where I go so the people there don't get to know me. I eat everything and then go throw up somewhere, all before I get home. Then I walk in the door like nothing ever happened.*

*I throw up in little plastic bags and I keep them under my bed. Then, when my mom is gone, I take them out to the garbage. If she found out, I'd die.*

## Doesn't She Know it's Not Good for Her?

Often, someone with bulimia is fully aware that bingeing and purging is dangerous and damaging to her body. At times this knowledge may frighten her, at others she may feel invincible. But usually her need for the eating disorder is so great that she doesn't care about potential consequences.

*I have little cavities in my teeth, which I heard was from purging, from the stomach acid.*

*I recently had a bone density test and it wasn't good. My bones are only as strong as an 80-year-old woman. You'd think that would make me stop, wouldn't you? But it doesn't.*

*I think it has ruined my health in a lot of ways. I think it's aged my body. I feel older than I really am.*

*I have so messed myself up from all the laxatives, now my body doesn't work right. I guess I should have thought of that before. But I didn't think this would happen to me.*

*I am tired all the time, and I get tired quicker. I have really dry skin. I mean, my face gets swollen and there are just physical things. I have had tons of dental work, and now I've managed to wear the enamel off my teeth. I also have scarring on the back of my hand that won't go away.*

*At this point I really can't keep anything down. It's funny, I tried for so many years to throw everything up, and now it just happens, even when I don't want it to.*

*People tell me I'm ruining my body. I don't believe it. None of those things are going to happen to me. I'm stronger than that.*

## What Other Behaviors Are Associated with Bulimia?

As opposed to anorexia, a disorder in which an individual typically keeps a tight and calculated reign over her actions, bulimia is characterized by impulsivity. Other impulsive behaviors sometimes used by people with bulimia include drug or alcohol abuse, cutting or burning oneself, obsessively studying or working, promiscuous sexuality, and stealing.

*Home life was a mess. My mom and I fought all the time. I felt trapped in my sad mind and body. So as a way of dealing with it, I began drinking a lot. I started cutting on myself and had a lot of strange sexual experiences.*

*When I start to cut or burn, I just go numb. Sometimes I can go numb just thinking about doing it. It feels so still, so calm.*

*I don't know why I did it, but I got into stealing. It wasn't like I needed any of the stuff I took. We weren't poor... I could have bought any of it. But I got some kind of rush. It was a challenge, and I felt a high when I got away with it. It's funny, I think of myself as a moral person, so I couldn't believe I was doing this.*

*When I was doing drugs, I did it like every night for months. . . I loved the drugs. I loved everything about them because not only was I thin, I was more confident when high on them than I have ever been. I wasn't insecure about anything. In fact, insecurity seemed ridiculous. I just felt good all the time.*

*I go out every weekend and get bombed. I drink as much as I can. I eat too. The drinking makes purging easier. And all of it makes me not care about anything.*

Also typical in bulimia are attempts to *restrict* food intake, at least some of the time, because it is a way of avoiding bingeing and purging. Limiting what she eats helps her feel more in control or more disciplined. She sees it as "pure" and "clean" and something to be admired, as opposed to bingeing and purging which she views as out of control and something to be reviled.

*I am so afraid to gain weight from bingeing, so I basically don't eat the rest of the time.*

*I try so hard to diet. I just don't have the willpower. I always end up bingeing.*

*I know I should eat, but I can't. But I know what happens. . . I just make myself more hungry, and then I have to binge.*

*If I binge and purge, then I have to diet the rest of the week.*

## Callista's Story

As in the chapter on anorexia, we offer the story of a young woman, this time one who suffers from bulimia. And, as before, although she and her life are unique, elements of her struggle may be applicable to yours.

### I'm Callista

Callista grew up in a family with two younger brothers and both parents, all of whom she considered her "best friends." They spent lots of time together, much of it traveling, which Callista liked.

Callista began making herself throw up at age 13 for reasons that were not clear to her at the time. She later reflected that, "It just seemed like the right thing to do for some reason." She wouldn't have described herself as depressed or upset. She had good friends and school was "fine." Soon, though, she began eating less and purging more often, sometimes two or three times a day. She also started running several miles on a daily basis.

When she was about 14, Callista resolved to restrict her eating habits even more. She felt "fat and out of control with my food," and thought she would feel better if she only ate an apple for breakfast and was "really careful" the rest of the day. She began to throw away her school lunch and to avoid eating dinner with her family, while simultaneously increasing her exercise regimen.

> I joined the basketball team at school to make it look like I was just a
> normal kid, just wanting to do school sports. But I knew perfectly well what
> I was after was burning calories, nothing else. I didn't even like basketball,
> but that didn't matter. All that mattered was losing weight.

During this time, she began to binge on large quantities of food, which she often meticulously planned. She did it when no one was around or after everyone had gone to sleep, since at these times there was less chance of getting caught. When she binged, Callista would eat "anything in the house." She often ate all the leftovers from dinner, or she would make cookies or pies then devour virtually all of them herself. Sometimes she baked two batches so her family wouldn't recognize what she was doing.

> I would make two of everything. Then I could eat an entire batch myself and
> they wouldn't be suspicious, since there would be plenty left for them.

Callista either ate alone in the kitchen or in her bedroom where she could eat without anyone knowing. After she had "eaten all I could fit into my stomach," she would go into the bathroom, turn on the shower to make noise, and purge. Sometimes she threw up into plastic bags and hid them in her room until they could be secretly discarded.

At this point in her life, "All I could think about was bingeing and purging." Her relationships with friends began to deteriorate and she spent more and more time on her own.

> I couldn't think of anything to talk to my friends about. I had this big secret life, and what was I supposed to say? "Hey, guess what I do in my spare time? Eat a lot and make myself throw up!" They would have thought I was crazy. Besides, they were talking about boys and clothes and stuff, and my thoughts were so not on those. I didn't care about any of that.

Despite a loss of about ten pounds, Callista remained at a relatively average weight. Still, her parents were alarmed by the changes in her behavior regarding friends and eating and worried she might continue to try to lose weight. Although the family physician found nothing medically wrong with her, she did suggest that her parents watch for the development of an eating disorder. Callista was relieved she "hadn't been found out" and therefore wouldn't have to make any changes in her behavior. At the least, she had anticipated the doctor would tell her not to exercise so much.

Near the end of her freshman year at high school, Callista felt left out and disliked by her friends. Concentrating on and finishing her schoolwork had become almost impossible and her grades suffered, which left Callista disappointed and frustrated with herself.

> I didn't understand how things could have gone so wrong. My life was going along so well and everything was under control, and now it was starting to fall apart. It was spiraling out of my control and I didn't know what to do. I clung to the eating disorder even more.

As Callista's depression and anxiety increased, she discovered *cutting*, a severe form of self-inflicted harm, and began practicing it on herself. She couldn't say exactly how she fell upon the behavior, but once she found it, she couldn't stop, not unlike her experience with purging.

> I liked cutting because I didn't have to deal with eating too much or throwing it up or worrying about gaining weight, and I could hide the cutting. And my parents were totally on my case about eating, anyway. They

*thought I was getting too skinny and they were threatening to take me back to the doctor.*

Cutting became a new-found obsession. Although she continued to binge and purge on a lesser scale, Callista's main focus was how to get away from people so she could cut herself, sometimes fantasizing about it all day.

*I'm sure people would have been freaked if they knew. My parents would have thought I was trying to kill myself. I wasn't at all though. Cutting gave me that same feeling I had when I purged ... like a high, and like nothing could harm me. I felt so okay when I did it. Nothing else mattered. I didn't care about anything.*

She worked hard to keep her this a secret. Like bingeing and purging, she didn't think anyone would understand. For several months she did manage to conceal the behavior by making incisions only on her abdomen and upper legs. Cautious dressing was essential, as any wounds or scars had to be covered.

But one morning, before Callista had dressed herself, her mother spotted some of the cuts. Callista was horrified she had been discovered, and her parents were alarmed their daughter would do something so harmful to herself. They immediately called their doctor and got the name of a psychotherapist who specialized in treating eating disorders and self-harm behaviors.

## The Reasons for Callista's Bulimia

Even Callista was baffled as to why she had started to binge and purge and cut herself. She couldn't come up with any reasons that made any sense to her. She thought the behaviors began randomly, that she had stumbled upon them by chance.

*Everyone kept asking me, but I didn't know why. I mean, I got it that most people don't do those things, but I had to do them. And the longer I did them the more attached to it all I became.*

Talking about her life to a counselor was difficult. She wasn't comfortable being the center of attention and usually tried to deflect conversations away from herself. But the more familiar she became with her therapist, the easier it became.

After several months, Callista experienced a breakthrough when she confessed to her therapist that an older male relative had molested her when she was 12 years old. At the time it had happened, she didn't say anything to anyone, believing she had "asked for it" by being alone with him and worrying her parents would say it was her fault or think she was "disgusting." In addition, this particular relative was very well-liked and she presumed her family wouldn't believe he was capable of such a horrific act. Lastly, she was afraid that the disclosure might cause irreparable conflict and disarray in her family, a risk she was unwilling to take.

At this point, although she thought it was too late to speak to her parents about the incident, she did acknowledge how frightening and confusing the assault had been. She finally realized she had been depressed and anxious for a very long time, but had tried earnestly to pretend she was fine. She did it so well that she even managed to convince herself she was happy.

It wasn't long after the molestation that Callista started purging. Thanks to therapy, she recognized bingeing and purging helped her avoid admitting what happened with her relative. Bingeing, throwing up, fasting, and cutting allowed her to be distracted and avoid painful memories. She had no time to think about anything else. And, best of all, the behaviors left her feeling "high" and invulnerable, as if no further harm could come to her.

Callista was ashamed about what her relative did to her and felt it made her a "bad person." Therefore she remained silent, feeling increasingly alone and becoming more isolated from the people around her. While her friends' interests were clothes and boys, she couldn't relate to those things anymore. Furthermore, she didn't see how "bringing up the molestation could do any good for anyone. It would just cause a mess. With my friends, with my family."

When her parents first took Callista to see the doctor, she feared she would be forced to change her behavior. This terrified her, because restricting food and bingeing and purging had become her sole coping strategy.

> *I didn't know why at the time, but I felt like I would die if they made me stop purging or made me eat more. I didn't know what else to do.*

Cutting provided another coping mechanism for her. Whenever she cut herself, she felt "numb, like I was rubber." By cutting, she didn't have to feel the shame, confusion, and fear that pervaded her life and psyche. Furthermore, cutting provided a special benefit, as far as she was concerned.

> *I got to feel like I was punishing myself. Purging sort of did that too…the more harsh I could be on myself the better. But cutting really did it. I could see the blood, and the next day it would really hurt.*

> *I thought I should be punished for what had happened with him. I was thinking, if I could just punish myself enough I'd feel better, that it would all go away.*

Of course, despite restricting her food, bingeing and purging, and cutting, "it all didn't go away." In treatment Callista began to truly resolve her feelings about being molested, to understand it was not her fault, and that she wasn't a bad or disgusting person. She also discovered that her emotions were important teachers and adopted other ways to cope with them that didn't involve bulimia or cutting.

**PART III**

{ *Supporting Their Recovery* }

**CHAPTER 6**

# Treatments for Eating Disorders

## *Where Do We Go From Here?*

Your loved one has finally admitted she has an eating disorder. What's the next step? Whom do you call? How do you get her the help she needs?

These are difficult questions, and the answers depend greatly on her current physical condition and the severity of her eating disorder. The appropriate course of action for some individuals might be outpatient psychotherapy, while others might need immediate medical care and/or hospitalization.

Anorexia and bulimia are extremely complicated, and treating them is an area of specialty. Ideally, your loved one should see a physician who has been trained to deal with these illnesses. Starting with your primary care physician is fine. However, if that doctor doesn't have the training or experience to help, he or she should then refer her to someone who does (for referral services, see Helpful Organizations).

# The First Step: Appointment with a Physician

Proper medical care is a *must* for someone with an eating disorder. This is true whether or not your loved one looks or feels sick, since these illnesses can take an enormous toll on one's health without apparent symptoms.

If your loved one is under 18 years of age, and therefore a minor, the first step is to make an appointment with your family physician or her pediatrician. You can accompany her to the appointment, but be aware doctors vary in ways they involve parents. Some may have you join her in the exam room, while others will evaluate her alone, the hope being she might then feel more comfortable and as a result be more honest about what she is experiencing.

If you do accompany your child for the exam, allow her to speak first so she has the opportunity to ask questions or offer her own perspective. Also, allow her to answer the doctor's questions in her own words. Resist the temptation to jump in and offer your viewpoint. Wait until you are asked a question or she's unable to provide specific information. Respect the fact that your loved one might feel ashamed or upset because you're in the room with her. If you won't be present during the exam but want to speak with the doctor, request a chance to come in for a few minutes after the evaluation is completed.

If she is 18 or older, the first step is to strongly, but gently, encourage her to make an appointment herself. You don't necessarily get to go with her, but you can certainly ask if she'd like you to accompany her for support. You must accept the fact that she may not want you to be there, and this is her decision.

During this first medical appointment, the physician will assess her physical condition and need accurate information to make a thorough evaluation. Here are the main things the physician will want to know:

- when the symptoms began or were first noticed

- amount and level of exercise per day, if any

- degree of food restriction (remember, someone with an eating disorder will have a tendency to overestimate the amount of food she is actually consuming)

- if there has been weight loss, how much and over what period of time

- frequency of bingeing and purging (remember, someone with an eating disorder will have a tendency to underestimate the frequency of these behaviors)

- regular use of laxatives, diet pills, or diuretics, or any other chemicals, drugs, medications, or alcohol

- loss of menstruation and when it first occurred

- dizziness, light-headedness, or fainting; racing or irregular heart beat

- any other symptoms you may have noticed or your loved one has complained about (e.g., constipation, hair loss, bruises easily, accelerated tooth decay, heartburn)

If you are accompanying a minor to the doctor it may well be you who communicates most effectively with the physician, as youngsters (particularly ones who are burdened with an eating disorder) might not be capable of answering extensive questions or even have the vocabulary to articulate this kind of information. Even if your loved one is an adult, she may benefit from your assistance in preparing information and formulating detailed, helpful answers.

This first evaluation may be quite difficult for your loved one. She may feel exposed, vulnerable, embarrassed, humiliated, annoyed, unwilling, or frightened. She may not want to be at the appointment. She might still be in denial and not even believe she needs help at this point. Often, she will be angry at or feel betrayed by whoever made the appointment.

*I couldn't believe they made me go. I felt like if they really loved me, they wouldn't make me do it. I hated them at first. I couldn't believe it was for my own good.*

*I was SO scared. I didn't know what was going to happen. I thought it might be something bad and harmful. My mom didn't know what was going to happen either, so she couldn't help me be less scared.*

*I was so mad. The doctor asked me if I was purging, and I said no. Then my mother told him that she knew I was throwing up. I couldn't believe she said that. It wasn't until months later that I forgave her and could see that she was only trying to help so he would know the truth.*

Keep in mind how stressful it can be for someone with anorexia or bulimia to open up to others. She might feel threatened, as if you or the doctor is trying to "take away" the disorder before she is "ready." Remember, she views it as her best friend and you are, in effect, attempting to end this relationship.

Your loved one might also have difficulty describing her true experience. As we've said, she may not be able to identify physical symptoms and may not be aware of her emotions. Sometimes family members make the mistake of interpreting this difficulty speaking about herself as being "bratty," "resistant," or "stubborn." While this might be the case, many times she really is in the dark about what's happening to her.

*I didn't know what to say to the doctor. She asked me all kinds of questions, but it didn't make any sense to me. I didn't think anything was wrong. I didn't think I needed to be there.*

## Be Prepared at the Doctor's Office

As we've mentioned, your loved one will preferably meet with professionals who have extensive experience working with eating disorders. A first appointment with a family physician who is sensitive to her situation can set the stage for future success.

*It actually turned out to be a relief. The doctor knew what he was talking about, and I could ask him tons of questions. He didn't make fun of me like I thought he was going to. I ended up not feeling so alone.*

*The doctor was so great. She was nice and seemed to know exactly what to say. I was really scared going the first time, but she made me feel less afraid.*

However, depending on where you live or other factors, finding someone with experience may not be an option. If your loved one happens to consult a professional who doesn't specialize in these disorders, she (and you) should be prepared in case the practitioner or a staff member says something unintentionally thoughtless or inappropriate. The likelihood is that they are unaware of the seriousness of eating disorders and might not even realize something objectionable was said.

*The medical assistant told me as she was weighing me that I didn't look anorexic. As soon as she said that to me, I knew I wasn't going to eat that day.*

*She just looked at me and asked why I was there. I told her that I had bulimia, and she just looked at me and said, "What do you think I can do about that?" I felt like an idiot, like I should've never gone and that I was wasting her time.*

*The doctor said to me, "Why don't you just binge on carrots? They don't have any calories, so you wouldn't have to throw up." I was thinking, he so does not get this at all. I'm not ever going to tell him anything.*

If a situation like this does occur, speak up. It could be a learning opportunity for everyone involved, medical community included! Also, if you are not satisfied with a particular doctor or caregiver, continue to shop around until you find just the right fit.

After this initial appointment, the next step is to choose an individual psychotherapist or a program which specializes in the treatment of eating disorders.

# The Treatment Team

Whether you choose an individual therapist or an eating disorder program, most treatment for anorexia or bulimia is a team effort so that your loved one will have multiple levels of support. A treatment team generally consists of a group of professionals who have different areas of expertise, working together to stabilize the disorder and helping your loved one begin the recovery process. It usually includes a psychotherapist (e.g., psychologist, social worker, master's level therapist, or counselor), a dietitian, and a physician.

## The Psychotherapist

Each clinician on the treatment team has his or her own unique and crucial role to play. The therapist is usually the "leader" of the team, primarily because eating disorders are largely psychological disturbances, which means he or she will have the most consistent contact with your loved one. In addition to working directly with the patient on issues related to her illness, the role of team leader is to ensure continuous and accurate communication as well as coordinate treatment goals amongst the various care providers.

Many types of therapists with varying levels of education and expertise are qualified to treat individuals with eating disorders, including (but not limited to) psychologists (PhD, PsyD, EdD), master's level therapists (MSW, MFCC, MA, MS), social workers (LCSW, LISW), and professional counselors (such as addiction counselors). Additionally, psychiatrists, who are medical doctors (MDs), can provide psychotherapy as well as prescribe medication.

However, in most cases the type of degree or license a therapist holds is not as important as his or her training and experience treating individuals and families who have struggled with eating disorders. Equally important is that there be good rapport between your loved one and the therapist with whom she chooses to work.

The job of the therapist is to help your loved one understand, acknowledge, and resolve the issues that are fueling her illness. Together they will investigate what conditions most likely caused the eating disorder and what beliefs and values support it. They will explore topics related to power and control, feelings of self-worth and self-esteem, and emotional experiences in general. Ultimately, they will work cooperatively to find and develop healthier coping skills so your loved one doesn't need to rely on her disorder to deal with her life. Achieving these goals will at times be challenging and a lengthy process, but full recovery from anorexia or bulimia demands dedication by everyone involved.

## The Dietitian

Initially, the role of the dietitian is to stabilize your loved one's nutrition. Someone with an eating disorder often knows a great deal about food (such as its calorie and fat content or the percentage of carbohydrates) but has a very difficult time putting this information to use in a healthy way. In fact, she'll tend to use her knowledge *against* herself much of the time. In addition, she'll have many ideas about nutrition that are erroneous.

> *I've heard that people eat way too much fat, so I'm just being healthy.*

> *I've read that too much protein isn't good for you.*

> *I know if you eat after 5 p.m. you store it all as fat.*

> *All foods that are cooked are bad for you. All white foods too.*

> *If you eat fat, it goes straight to your body and lodges there. I can almost see that cheese I ate this morning right on my thigh.*

Later on, the dietitian will develop a nutritional plan that meets your loved one's needs and begins to stabilize her body chemistry. What's more, your loved one should be invited to contribute to the creation of this plan because the more involved (and therefore powerful and in control) she feels about the food arrangement, the more likely she will be to agree and attempt to follow it.

As recovery progresses and the treatment relationship becomes stronger, the dietitian will begin to confront the myths and misunderstandings your loved one has about food. This will enable the reintroduction of foods she has considered "unsafe" and has been afraid to eat. The eventual nutritional goal is for her to be able to listen to what her body needs and wants, and to choose what she eats according to those signals instead of basing her nutritional decisions on distorted beliefs dictated by the eating disorder.

## The Physician

As mentioned earlier, the initial job of the physician is assessment. This treatment team member also has an important ongoing responsibility, which is to monitor the patient to make sure she remains medically stable. This includes routinely checking things such as heart rate and blood pressure, as well as keeping an eye on potassium and other electrolyte levels. The more serious the eating disorder, the more closely the doctor will need to monitor her physical condition.

No matter what medical state your loved one is in, a physician should always be involved. This may be the same person you originally consulted (your family physician), one who works closely with your chosen therapist, or the resident doctor at a treatment facility. Often, the doctor is a psychiatrist—a medical doctor who has completed a three- to five-year psychiatric residency and has specialized training in the most appropriate and effective medications.

Medication may be necessary either for the short term to facilitate treatment or for the long run to achieve emotional balance. Examples of commonly prescribed drugs include Prozac, Paxil, Effexor and Lexapro, to name a few. These and other regularly used medications aim to relieve depression, anxiety, or a combination of both. The need to prescribe medication is one of the reasons why you and your loved one need to feel especially comfortable with and confident in her physician.

Based on her overall health, the doctor will determine the frequency of appointments. If she is experiencing any physical complications from her eating disorder, such as lightheadedness, dizziness or fainting, lowered body temperature, or too slow a heart rate, she will have to be more closely monitored. Over time, as your loved one develops a relationship with her doctor, you will be able to rest assured that a medical professional with an enduring interest is watching her and will catch any physical changes that might occur.

## Choosing Professional Help

When considering professionals to work with your loved one, you need to interview them. Don't be shy, and don't be in a hurry and settle for just anyone. Some therapists offer an initial free consultation so that all parties can get to know each other, without making a commitment, and decide if they want to work together. As we emphasize throughout this book, treating someone with anorexia, bulimia, or related symptoms requires specialized knowledge and skill. Make sure that the person who's going to be treating your loved one has adequate experience and expertise.

Here are some types of questions you might want to ask:

- What's your philosophy about what causes an eating disorder and how someone recovers from one? Not all professionals hold the same beliefs, and therefore use different methods for treatment; it's important to work with people she feels have a similar perspective so she can relate to and feel comfortable with them.

- How do you feel about working with other professionals? Is working as a member of a treatment team the typical way you work, and, if not, in what way do you work and why?

- How long have you treated people with eating disorders? What is your success rate?

- What specialized training have you had?

- What percentage of the people you treat have eating disorders?

- What resources would you use if my loved one requires a higher level of care at some point?

You can, of course, ask anything else you're curious about. Feel free to bring up any subjects or concerns that you consider relevant. Your loved one's physical and emotional health are at risk, and this is not the time to have any doubts.

Rely on people you trust to guide you toward help, such as your family physician or someone you know who has successfully recovered from an eating disorder. There are also several reputable organizations dedicated to directing families toward effective and useful resources (see Helpful Organizations).

## Levels of Care

There are several levels of care for treating eating disorders. Here, we describe each of them and tell you how to judge which might be most appropriate for your situation.

All these approaches, except hospitalization, allow your loved one to immediately practice in the outside world what she learns in treatment. This is important because it's one thing to *learn* new ways of being in the world, and another to *apply* them to daily life.

## Basic Outpatient Treatment

The most common place for someone to begin is called outpatient treatment. This level of care is appropriate for a person who is medically stable (meaning she doesn't need immediate emergency medical attention or to be admitted into a hospital) and is able to function fairly well in her life even though she has an eating disorder.

This counseling does not necessarily take place in a facility or in a specialized program. Sometimes good outpatient care can be accomplished with a single therapist in an office setting. No matter what the location, though, the therapist is usually the hub of a treatment team and will coordinate communication between its members.

An example of this level of care would be one or more individual therapy sessions, of about an hour each, every week, along with supplemental appointments with a dietitian or psychiatrist. Additionally, the therapist may offer or recommend group therapy or family therapy.

## Group Therapy

Someone with anorexia or bulimia often feels alone, as if no one else is feeling what she feels. Joining a support group with others who also have eating disorders provides a means to feel connected, to see she isn't "the only one" or "a freak," and to relate to people who are suffering in similar ways.

Group therapy might be offered by her individual counselor or through established organizations with local branches, such as the National Association of Anorexia Nervosa & Associated Disorders (ANAD), *www.anad.org,* or Eating Disorders Anonymous (EDA), *www.eatingdisordersanonymous.org.*

> *I'm shy and I didn't want to be in a group. But they were all just like me. It made it easy to fit in there.*

> *I didn't have to explain much. I could just say a few words and everyone would nod like, "Oh yeah, I get it."*

> *I couldn't talk to anyone, not my family or friends. I had all these secrets. Group gave me a place to tell the truth.*

## Family Therapy

Because an eating disorder affects the entire family, everyone who is closely involved with the sufferer can benefit from professional help and support. Parents, siblings, and significant others often have many questions and concerns, and they too need someone to talk to and somewhere to go for comfort, accurate information, and answers to their queries.

Family therapy is highly recommended because sometimes families fail to see how they might be contributing to the problem, or that they can be part of the solution. Family therapy is not about assigning blame, it's about learning new ways to communicate, support, and respect each other, and it will help everyone involved.

> *We were so afraid. We thought we were to blame for her illness and that we had ruined her in some way. We needed a lot of help to understand the way our family worked, and didn't work. We finally came to understand that we did have a part in why she had gotten sick, but it wasn't that we had set out to harm her, or that we meant for this to happen.*

> *She always had worried about our marriage. We tried to convince her that things were okay, but she still worried. It was like she was trying to take care of us and make sure we were okay. We all had to figure out different ways of being together.*

> *Her mother had such difficulty expressing herself. And I am a pretty open person. We have very different ways of dealing with the world. These differences affected our daughter more than we had realized. We never imagined they might have something to do with her eating disorder.*

> *There was a lot of competition between her and her sisters. We never understood that. All three of them are such terrific girls. And we didn't see it, that it had to do with us in any way. We all had to learn to understand what this competitive stuff meant in our family and then to deal with it. It was tough, but we're glad we did it. It's given our whole family a lot more freedom, and we are a lot closer now.*

## Intensive Outpatient Programs

The next level of care is an intensive outpatient program (IOP), which typically consists of at least three hours of structured treatment per day, provided at a specialized institution. This is a good choice if your loved one tries a less-rigorous outpatient treatment plan but finds it doesn't quite impart enough support or structure for her to make positive changes in her eating behaviors.

IOPs can either replace or be combined with a basic outpatient treatment plan. They provide some combination of individual and family psychotherapy, group therapy, support to help educate families about eating disorders, and nutritional counseling. As with standard outpatient treatment, the IOP team typically consists of a psychotherapist, family therapist, medical practitioner and dietitian. Often there are other clinicians, such as an art, music, or drama therapist.

Remember that someone participating in intensive outpatient programs needs to be medically stable because these programs aren't equipped to provide intensive medical supervision. For this reason, people in IOPs need to continue seeing an outside physician.

## Day-Treatment Programs

A more comprehensive level of care is a day-treatment or partial hospitalization. This type of treatment offers full-day support, typically six to eight hours per day, usually five days a week, with the patient returning home each night to sleep. The amount of time spent directly in treatment (number of hours per day as well as number of days per week at the program) is what differentiates day-treatment from intensive outpatient treatment.

Day-treatment programs offer a variety of group therapies during the day, as well as several structured meals. Individual therapy, nutritional counseling, and often a family component are included.

## Inpatient or Residential Treatment

Inpatient or residential treatment is where your loved one lives at the treatment facility full time. These programs are for those who do not need acute medical care, but who require constant supervision and structure as determined by a physician. Unlike less-intensive levels of care, your loved one lives at the facility 24 hours a day, for as little as four weeks to as long as several months or more.

The inpatient environment is best for individuals who cannot gain weight by themselves, have not been able to alter their eating-disordered behaviors in outpatient settings, or need to be supported and observed during and after all meals. Programs like these can be either hospital-based or exist as a non-medical facility designed to be a safe and comfortable setting that provides all necessary medical and psychological support.

Some inpatient programs cater exclusively to individuals with eating disorders, while others include people with drug or alcohol, or psychiatric problems. In general, the best course of action is to choose a program that has been specifically designed for those who have eating disorders. However, in some cases you might elect to use a facility that offers treatment for a variety of issues. This might be the case, for example, if your loved one has other problems to work on in addition to her anorexia or bulimia, if an exclusively eating-disorders program isn't available in your area, or if the ones that do exist cannot accept your type of insurance.

## What Happens Each Day?

Days are filled with various types of psychotherapy, primarily group therapy, as well as individual counseling. As always, families are encouraged to participate. Food and exercise are strictly monitored, at least in the beginning stages. As the patient gets stronger, she is allowed more flexibility and choice regarding what and how much she eats and works out.

This method of treatment temporarily removes your loved one from the family or her home. Although inpatient treatment can be very challenging at first, it does provide the patient with the opportunity to focus completely on her recovery without the distractions of daily living, such as school, work, or socializing.

## What Happens When She Gets Better?

As she gets close to completing her stay as an inpatient, the treatment team and the facility's staff, in conjunction with you and your loved one, will decide what is the next step in her recovery. She might be ready to return home and begin outpatient treatment, or it might be best for her to transition to day-treatment or an intensive outpatient program instead. Many inpatient facilities offer a *step down* program, which is day-treatment followed by an intensive outpatient program, with all services located at the same center.

## Medical Hospitalization

The most acute level of care is medical hospitalization. Typically, this is advised when your loved one's physical health is significantly compromised and she needs immediate medical attention. In most cases, the hospitalization is relatively short term, with the focus on rehydration (getting her body's fluids back to normal levels), refeeding (getting her to begin eating on a regular basis, or eating without vomiting), and medical stabilization (maintaining vital signs within a relatively normal range). A physician who has been continuously monitoring and observing your loved one's condition during her treatment is the one who will determine if and when medical hospitalization is necessary.

Once your loved one is discharged from the hospital she'll begin or return to her usual treatment routine. In some cases, several medical hospitalizations may be necessary before the individual's health becomes consistently stabilized.

## Reassessing Treatment

Your loved one's therapeutic needs will change over time as she progresses on the road to recovery. Certainly, all treatment decisions can and should be reevaluated periodically. Such reassessment will be done collaboratively between your loved one and her treatment team, often with input from you, based on your evaluation of how things are improving.

Remember that no choice is written in stone. If, after your loved one has worked with a particular practitioner, treatment team, or level of care, she is not responding or wants to try something different, she certainly can and should. However, any changes to her treatment protocol need to be discussed carefully and thoughtfully with her current caregivers, whose goal should be finding viable and practical alternatives.

**CHAPTER 7**

# The Phases of Recovery

## *What Should We Expect?*

Recovering from an eating disorder is a process, and each phase has different challenges and rewards. In this chapter, we describe these phases, help you understand what they entail, and give you some idea of what to expect along the way. To best illustrate the process, we follow two women on their journey through treatment and ultimate success.

Identifying the phases of recovery can be extremely beneficial for both the individual with the eating disorder and her family. Although the parameters of each stage are somewhat broad, they do offer a basic framework for treatment, as well as help your loved one pace herself and anticipate what might happen next. Achieving milestones can help her (and you) see how much progress has actually occurred.

Keep in mind that although most people go through some variation of these stages, every individual must follow her own unique path. A crucial aspect of resolving an eating disorder is uncovering and *recovering* one's passion for life and living. What's inspiring for one person may not be useful for another.

Furthermore, recovery is not a straight line; sometimes your loved one might appear to take one step forward and two steps back. You may worry when this happens, fearing the disease has once again taken hold. However, temporary setbacks are a normal part of the process. What's important is an overall trend toward getting better.

Your loved one may experience periods when she feels hopeful and elated followed by phases where she becomes terribly frustrated and wants to give up. These are the times when your presence will be of greatest value to her. She'll need constant help to maintain the perspective that things *can* and *will* get better.

# Phase One: Stabilization

The first phase of recovery begins when your loved one enters treatment. During this initial stage, she will meet and begin working with the core members of her treatment team. The specific team members and the level of care may need adjustment during the course of treatment, but the main components are established at this time.

The primary goal during this phase is to stop the progression of the illness to prevent her condition from worsening. The secondary goal is to begin to *reverse* the course of the disorder. In order to achieve this, several aspects of stabilization may need to be addressed, including medical, psychological, behavioral, and nutritional.

## Medical Stabilization

If an individual is significantly underweight, severely malnourished, and/or experiencing medical complications, she simply will not be able to think clearly or rationally. If your loved one enters treatment in such a state, most of the first phase will focus on improving and stabilizing her physical condition and weight so that successful psychological work can take place at a later date.

For someone who has anorexia, medical stabilization is achieved when she has gained sufficient weight to be out of acute medical danger, and her vital signs (such as heart rate, blood pressure, and body temperature) and electrolyte levels (determined through blood tests) become reasonably consistent and stable.

An individual with bulimia is considered medically stable when her vital signs are reliably within a normal range and her purging is infrequent enough that it doesn't cause her to become seriously dehydrated or her electrolyte levels to become unbalanced.

Becoming medically stable does not mean the individual is totally out of the woods or that she'll never be in acute medical danger during the course of treatment. As stated previously, recovery is not a straight line and there may be critical setbacks. However, getting through these initial physical challenges is a very important first step. Potential fluctuations in your loved one's health also underscore the need for a medical doctor to be a member of the core team.

## Psychological Stabilization

There are several areas that need to be tackled in order to achieve basic psychological stabilization, including managing any existing depression or anxiety, changing thought processes, developing insight, and improving communication.

Some individuals know that they suffer from depression and/or anxiety before they begin a program, whereas others may not realize it until they are diagnosed while in treatment. Although rare, not everyone with an eating disorder suffers from anxiety or depression. But when these conditions interfere with the ability to focus on or understand treatment, addressing them must be an immediate goal.

Depression and anxiety may be handled in various ways. Medication (generally antidepressants) can be quite valuable, as can learning and using various coping techniques (for example, meditation or guided imagery) offered in therapy. Sometimes just the relief of having found people to help and knowing she is now on a healing path can alleviate some of the anxious feelings your loved one may be experiencing.

Also in this phase, the treatment team will help her begin to gain insight into the causes and meaning behind her behaviors and the purpose they serve in her life. She'll be introduced to alternative methods that offer her a choice: she can either continue her eating-disordered behaviors for help dealing with a given situation or she can try new strategies. Her emerging ability to make this kind of decision isn't the complete answer to her eating disorder, but it is a first, important step.

Developing and working on communication skills, as well as gaining confidence in her ability to use them, can be invaluable at this time. For example, your loved one may want or need help composing and rehearsing her response when a friend, relative, teacher, or employer questions her about her eating disorder or treatment.

A good indicator that your loved one is moving toward psychological stabilization is that the eating-disordered thoughts and behaviors don't have such a tight grip on her. As she learns to addresses issues such as depression or anxiety, gains insight into her behaviors, and begins to develop ways to cope with her obsessive thoughts, she will gradually feel that her life is less chaotic and out-of-control. In fact, it is becoming more her own.

## Behavioral Stabilization

The behaviors of someone who is restricting, bingeing, or bingeing and purging can be so disruptive that they fill her day and cause her to feel like she's in a constant state of exhaustion. Therefore, curbing these behaviors so she can rest, both mentally and physically, is of primary concern.

Learning practical strategies, such as eating meals at regular times, not being alone after a meal, or talking with someone when she feels like bingeing, are examples of ways to start decreasing harmful behaviors. You and the treatment team need to encourage her to experiment with this process until she finds the strategies that work for her. If her first attempts aren't successful and she wants to give up, remind her that she hasn't failed and that recovery is a process.

## Nutritional Stabilization

A goal of this initial phase is to get your loved one to eat a sufficient and consistent amount of nutritious food. If she has anorexia, she needs help beginning to eat enough and on a regular basis; if she suffers from bulimia, she primarily needs help stabilizing her erratic eating patterns. A dietitian is key to this process because nutritional stabilization of someone who is used to starving or bingeing and/or purging is a complex process.

Her nutritional status and ongoing behaviors related to food will determine where she and her dietitian begin. Starting slowly and working together, they will gradually make changes in her food intake. Such a strategy gives her body, as well as her mind, a chance to get used to each adjustment. It also offers her an opportunity to learn coping strategies to handle the anxiety that eating in a new way will likely cause.

Your loved one may be put on a meal plan and have her caloric intake monitored by her dietitian. In this challenge, she may benefit from help from you or other people in her life. For example, sitting with her during meals can feel supportive, or participating in a joint activity after a meal limits her time alone. It is important to discuss any ideas like these in detail with her before implementing them. Whether or not she'll want you involved in food-related aspects of her life depends on many variables, including her age, current relationship with you, and where you live. How she wants you involved may change over time. This is an expected part of the recovery process and a sign of growth, not necessarily something to be concerned about.

## How Long Does the First Phase Last?

The first phase of recovery can last anywhere from a few weeks to several months or more, depending largely on how medically, nutritionally, and psychologically ill your loved one is when she begins treatment. In addition, the strength of her support system, her willingness, and her ability to make use of treatment will affect her capacity to take these first steps.

After achieving the stability of phase one, she will no longer feel as if she is living in a fog; her thinking will become clearer, and she will feel more in touch with her emotions and experiences. This will enable her to make much better use of any subsequent psychological treatment.

## What's it Like for Her?

Patients often feel a mix of emotions during this phase. Your loved one may feel powerless or overwhelmed by the process of recovery. She may be embarrassed or humiliated by her behavior. She might feel threatened by treatment. Even someone who *wants* to recover might fear what will happen if she (or anyone else) tries to eliminate her disorder because she "won't exist" without it or won't feel able to manage life on her own. Consequently, she may resist stabilization, feeling the need to cling to the safety and familiarity of her anorexia or bulimia.

These fears can manifest as defiance, rebelliousness, or anger, which can cause great frustration for her family and treatment team. You can help by listening carefully, and by reassuring her that her emotions are normal and that you understand how afraid she is. In Chapter 8 we'll talk about ways to take care of and support both your loved one and yourself throughout the challenging process of recovery.

Now we'll meet Karen and Mariko as each of them begins phase one of treatment for an eating disorder. We'll rejoin them later as they go through phases two and three of their journey to recovery.

## Karen's Recovery—Phase One

Karen's anorexia began just before her junior year in high school. Her parents became concerned about her low weight, but Karen insisted she was fine. Nonetheless, they made her see their family physician several times, but were repeatedly told it was nothing, just a harmless, girlish phase that would pass.

Several years later, at the beginning of her sophomore year at a local college, Karen's weight dropped significantly. Her grades were good, but it was apparent she wasn't having any fun at school and everything seemed hard for her. There were many family arguments about what to do; Karen's parents wanted her to take some time off from school to get healthier, but she was adamantly against that idea.

When Karen fainted on her way to class one day, the decision to get help was finally made. Her parents insisted she be evaluated at an inpatient eating-disorders facility. The assessment lasted several hours and within that time she met with a therapist, a nutritionist, a medical doctor, and a psychiatrist, all of whom agreed that Karen needed immediate medical care, largely because a full physical exam showed she was severely dehydrated.

Karen was terrified at the idea of being hospitalized. She feared she would be expelled from school and her life would be ruined. She was even *more* afraid that she would be forced to eat and, surely, that would be the end of her world.

Nonetheless, she was admitted to the program and immediately put on an intravenous drip to re-hydrate her body. She was prescribed bed rest for several days to ensure her medical safety. Four days later, she was stable enough to begin participating fully in the therapeutic aspects of the program.

For the first several weeks, Karen stubbornly maintained that nothing was wrong and she didn't need to be there. She was constantly angry, particularly with her parents. She struggled a great deal with eating, and at times the staff had to use a liquid supplement to meet her nutritional needs.

As the weeks progressed, though, she was able to eat more and more solid food, although her anxiety about eating and "getting fat" remained high. Karen also realized she was depressed, which was not unexpected. The anorexia had concealed her emotions for years, and when she began to get more nutritionally stable and clear-minded, they began to reveal themselves.

Beginning to feel her true emotions again was very distressing for Karen. She desperately wanted to return to starving herself, which she reluctantly acknowledged made her feel safe and in control. However, rather than revert to old behaviors, Karen was encouraged to discuss her fears about having emotions while participating in therapy. This slowly led her to identify and understand what anorexia meant to and did for her.

Karen's parents participated in weekly family therapy sessions while she was in treatment. Additionally, they attended support groups where they could share their experiences and emotions with other parents in similar situations.

Karen was an inpatient for about ten weeks, a period that constituted phase one of her treatment. She managed to gain enough weight so that she was no longer in medical danger, and her vital signs became acceptable and remained stable. She was still very frightened to eat, but now she could think more clearly because she was better nourished; she was able to reason with herself about how important it was to continue with treatment and her eating program.

## Mariko's Recovery—Phase One

Mariko, who suffered from bulimia since she was 15, entered treatment at age 25. For ten years she'd had managed to keep her eating disorder a secret from everyone she knew, including her entire family and fiancé. During those years she had felt too humiliated to get help; now she believed she "couldn't go on like this" anymore.

Although she had a full-time job and was surrounded by people who loved her, Mariko's life revolved around bingeing and purging. On a typical day, she would binge and purge three to five times, which left her feeling exhausted and weak.

When Mariko finally told her fiancé she needed help, they *both* went to a psychologist who specialized in treating eating disorders. The therapist agreed to work with Mariko, and then referred her to a dietitian and a medical doctor whom she saw within the next few weeks. The physician performed extensive blood work and an electrocardiogram (EKG) to see if Mariko's heart had suffered injury due to her disease. The various tests showed her electrolyte levels and blood pressure were low, but not dangerously so, and her heart activity was normal. The dietitian assessed Mariko's nutritional status and then formulated a nutritional plan to begin stabilizing her diet. Both the psychologist and medical doctor felt that although she might need more intensive care at some point, at the moment Mariko was healthy enough to participate in outpatient treatment.

Although she felt humiliated by having bulimia and "going public about it," Mariko was relieved to be getting help. "For the first time in years, I felt like there might be hope for me to get better." She continued with treatment consistently for the next six weeks. She worked very hard to follow her treatment team's advice but found it extremely difficult to make any changes in her bingeing and purging behavior. She had been doing it so long that she couldn't imagine stopping.

At her next medical check-up, the results of Mariko's lab tests indicated that her electrolyte levels had become out of balance, which indicated Mariko had possibly increased her binging and purging. More alarming was that her level of potassium was significantly low, which put her at much greater risk for medical complications, such as cardiac arrest, which causes the heart to suddenly stop beating. Her physician sent her to the emergency room to be re-hydrated, hoping this would increase her electrolytes to normal levels. She remained at the hospital for several hours and was not allowed to return home until the medical staff determined her condition was again stable and she was out of immediate danger.

Within a few days, however, Mariko's electrolyte levels were again out of range and her physician felt she was in sufficient medical danger to warrant admission to a medical unit for an extended period of time.

Although unhappy about it, Mariko agreed to be treated as an inpatient for five days. Because she was placed in a medical hospital, there was no therapy component during her stay. However, the nurses did sit with her during and after meals to assist her efforts to eat consistently and resist purging. Although it was hard at first, having trained staff around her 24 hours a day gave Mariko much-needed structure and support, which she eventually appreciated.

Mariko was considerably more stable when she was released from the hospital. As an inpatient, she had practiced eating without purging, and her electrolytes stayed within a normal range. Her team felt she was ready to continue to work on recovery as an outpatient.

Mariko decided to join a therapy group and increase her individual therapy appointments to twice a week. As a result, over the next few months, she managed to reduce her purging to less than twice a day, leaving her increasingly hopeful about her ability to recover. For Mariko, completing phase one meant reducing her unsafe food-related behaviors enough to allow her electrolyte levels to stay out of a dangerously low zone. Although she still participated in bingeing and purging, she felt she had greater control over these destructive behaviors and wasn't "spending all day thinking about my next binge."

## Phase Two: Exploring

Phase two is when the bulk of the psychological and behavioral work of recovery takes place. The main focus of treatment is no longer on crisis management and acute medical complications. Now that your loved one is physically stronger, she is able to think more clearly and make better use of treatment in general and therapy in particular.

Many individuals move from an inpatient to outpatient program at this time, if approved by their treatment team. No longer supported by the consistency of a structured setting, they will once again face life on their own. Re-adjusting to common events, such as buying, cooking, and eating food, scheduling appointments, enjoying free time, and interacting with family and friends, may prove to be challenging.

Outpatient treatment differs from inpatient in a variety of ways. An inpatient setting provides an enormous amount of structure and is contained under one roof. For the most part, the clinicians come *to* the patient. While certainly challenging in many respects, the inpatient setting provides shelter from the outside world and everything that goes with it. Staff and other patients are available on site for support, assistance, or therapy 24 hours a day.

However, in outpatient treatment, your loved one will likely travel to multiple locations to see her physician, psychotherapist, and dietitian. If age appropriate, *she* will be responsible for making and keeping her appointments: there will be no staff to remind her of therapy sessions. Outpatient treatment puts her back into "regular" life, where for the most part she will need to identify when she needs help and then ask for it.

The combination of regained personal responsibility and living her daily life while in recovery can make outpatient treatment at this stage somewhat complicated and demanding. Your loved one will likely need encouragement to reach out and communicate with people to avoid becoming isolated or withdrawn. She may even think she's weak or "failing at recovery" because the transition is difficult. You can help by reminding her you are there to support her and to listen. You can also acknowledge the significant differences between inpatient and outpatient treatment and acknowledge that returning home is an adjustment and can take some time.

*I had to go inpatient. I was so sick. But it was like being on a different planet for three months.*

*I liked the program. The structure was safe. I didn't have to plan anything. I just did what was next.*

*I call it "re-entry." The first few weeks after I got home was such a challenge! It was like I had to learn to do all these things over again. I mean, I hadn't even driven for months. Everything got easier after awhile, and I got more confident that I could do it.*

Your loved one's struggle with her disorder may reemerge or intensify during this transition. Such a development is not atypical, and it's important for everyone involved to be prepared in case it happens.

Psychological and emotional goals during this phase include gaining a deeper understanding of how the eating disorder functions in her life, identifying and resolving issues that underlie the disorder, and continuing to discover healthy ways to cope with her life so she doesn't feel the need to rely on starving herself or bingeing and purging.

During this stage of recovery she'll also work on her body image. She will learn to see her body objectively and realistically by eliminating mental distortions and accepting her body as it is, as opposed to how she thinks it "should be."

One related key development is making the connection between emotional issues and how she sees and feels about her body. For example, as she begins to understand that she feels especially fat when she is experiencing an uncomfortable emotion, she will be able to learn to reassure herself that she did not, in fact, suddenly gain ten pounds. Once that fact is understood and accepted, she will be better able to deal directly with the emotion she was originally having and will be more aware of her tendency to distract herself with negative body thoughts.

Behavioral goals during this phase depend on the type of eating disorder and condition of the individual. Someone who is underweight will need to continue to increase her weight until she reaches a more healthy range. Someone who binges and/or purges will need to understand her behaviors and their purposes, as well as to make significant reductions in the frequency they occur.

Nutritional goals during this phase include re-introducing challenging foods, those that she has labeled "unsafe" or "bad." She will also learn to trust that her body can tolerate a wide range of foods, and begin to make food choices based on physical rather than emotional hunger.

At times, the process of recovering from an eating disorder feels like a full-time job because it demands so much time and energy. For this reason, it may be hard or even impossible for your loved one to go to school or the workplace, at least during the first two phases of recovery.

On the other hand, having structure in her day (such as a schedule to keep or events to attend) and meaning in her life (like feeling she is contributing to the world in some way and "not just sitting around") can give her hope and keep her motivated. Decisions regarding jobs, volunteering, school, or any other activities, are complex and should be carefully thought through by the individual, her parents, and her team.

Let's rejoin the two women we met in phase one and see what phase two entailed for each of them.

## Karen's Recovery—Phase Two

Karen did very well as an inpatient. She enjoyed the structure it provided and learned to feel reasonably comfortable about eating in that type of environment. By the time she was discharged about ten weeks later her weight had stabilized and she was no longer in medical danger. She was, however, still somewhat underweight.

Before she was discharged, Karen and her team had set up an intensive outpatient plan where she would be receiving therapy roughly six hours per week, an enormous reduction from the 24-hour care and supervision she had while in the program. She liked her new treatment team, which consisted of a therapist, a dietitian, and a physician. She saw each of them two times a week, the plan being to reduce the number of visits as she became increasingly healthy. Every few weeks, her parents went for counseling with their own clinician who communicated with Karen's therapist. Doing so enabled her parents to get support, ask questions, and feel secure about how they were dealing with Karen's illness.

In therapy sessions, Karen discussed what she had learned about the eating disorder and its related behaviors, how she felt about recovery from anorexia, and what she wanted to change in her life to support those changes. It became clear to her during this time that she was afraid of living without the illness. She worried that, "I wouldn't know what to do. I'll be lost without it and just flail around in my life."

Karen was also encouraged to talk about her parents and her feeling that their marriage "was not really good at all." She thought her mother and father loved each other but they had "so many problems communicating and they are such different people; I don't see how they've even stayed together."

It emerged that Karen felt it was wrong to talk about these things, and she felt guilty when she admitted she thought her family had problems. Karen began to realize that she had *never* been honest about her home life, that she could only say "nice things" about her family, and that these factors most likely contributed to the development of her eating disorder.

> *I felt such pressure to always make everything look pretty, to make it look like we had the best family ever. In a lot of ways it was really good, and I'm grateful for that. I love my parents, and I know they love me. But we weren't—we aren't—perfect. So I felt like I was lying a lot. And I hated that. Maybe part of the way I dealt with the pressure was by not eating.*

She began to understand that growing up in a family where she constantly worried about the stability of her parents' marriage left her feeling insecure and "on edge" about life. It also made her feel things were always precarious, that maybe they would just disappear suddenly.

> *I worried a lot that out of the blue my parents would say they were getting divorced. And then, what would I have done? I was so afraid of that. All the time.*

Although Karen felt that her therapy was going well and she was making progress, the actual act of eating and accepting the resulting weight gain remained difficult. Many days she didn't want to eat at all, and her dietician struggled to get Karen to consume adequate nutrition. Her weight fluctuated somewhat, but it remained consistent enough to be of no medical worry, according to her doctor.

One important concern for Karen was her tendency to overexercise. While she was an inpatient, her activities had been assigned and closely monitored by the staff. Now that Karen was out of the program, *she* had to be in charge of how active she was.

> It was a constant battle for me. The anorexia kept saying, "You are SO fat and you need to go running." But then there was another part of me that said, "No, you need to get stronger before you can do that."

Karen recognized that too much activity would jeopardize her health, so with help from her treatment team, she committed to calling a friend or writing in her journal whenever she had the urge to overexercise. On days when she did too much, she would try to eat extra food to compensate for the increase in burned calories.

As Karen became stronger she found the courage to talk with her parents about her experience of growing up in a home where the father and mother did not get along with each other. She was fearful about telling them how she felt, but she realized that keeping her thoughts and emotions locked inside made her more prone to feel the need to restrict her food.

As it turns out, Karen's parents had no idea she was so deeply affected by their troubled relationship. Once they became aware, they apologized profusely for any suffering their discord may have caused and told her they would commit to couples counseling themselves.

In general, Karen liked the fact that she was getting stronger, but she still felt afraid. She was not yet convinced she wouldn't need anorexia to help her deal with life, and she seriously questioned whether she could manage without it. About eight months after leaving the inpatient program, her fears became particularly intense.

> I just felt I was getting so much closer to not having my anorexia. And while I was glad in some ways, I was also terrified. Actually, I really missed the

*disorder. I know it sounds weird, but it's true. Things seemed so clear and safe when I was really in the middle of it.*

Not surprisingly, Karen's weight began to drop at this time. She was overwhelmed by her worries about losing the disorder. She missed the days where she ate very little and seemed to have "the world in the palm of my hand." Her therapist assured her that many people feel the same way as they change their relationship with the eating disorder and that, although it was normal to miss things about the illness, she needed to stay on track if she wanted to recover.

Karen was relieved she wasn't "a freak", and that it didn't mean she secretly didn't want to get well. She continued to discuss the uncertainties of living without the disorder, and she allowed herself to accept the fact that there were certain aspects of it that she might always yearn to have again. She made an effort to find and include things in her life that helped her feel safe, secure, and powerful—the things the anorexia had provided her. Within a few weeks her good eating habits returned and her weight began to stabilize.

About 16 months after she was discharged from the hospital, Karen finally reached her goal weight range. Her menstrual cycle returned, and she felt stronger, healthier, and happier than she had in many years. By persevering and successfully completing phase two, Karen had developed a thorough understanding of what anorexia meant to her and how it served her life. She began to deal more directly with her emotions and issues, like her overwhelming familial relationships. Karen still needed support, but she was now ready for phase three of treatment and recovery.

## Mariko's Recovery—Phase Two

After several months of therapy, Mariko was making progress in her recovery. Even though she was still bingeing and purging at least once and sometimes twice a day, her eating was more stable than it had been in years, and she was taking in an adequate amount of nutrition. Her lab tests were consistently within normal range from week to week, which was reassuring to both her and her treatment team.

At one point, Mariko spontaneously divulged that she had been attacked and date-raped when she was 15 years old. Mariko had never told anyone about it because she, like many other girls, thought it was somehow her fault.

At last Mariko was able to connect this brutal event to the onset of her bulimia. Now she could begin to talk about all the emotions she had tried so desperately to bury: fear, anger, disgust, hopelessness, and helplessness. Her therapist helped her understand that she was not responsible for the assault, and had, in fact, done everything she could to get away from her attacker. Although Mariko was relieved to finally recount her rape, talking about it and feeling so many repressed emotions was intensely painful. As a consequence, she reverted back to old behaviors and began to binge and purge more frequently.

Because her symptoms were on the rise, Mariko and her family wondered if she was in fact getting worse. But Mariko's therapist assured her that the intensity of the emotions she was dealing with and her need to binge and purge were connected. Even though her outer symptoms were increasing, it was a temporary condition; she needed to continue working through the underlying issues of her disorder and that, while hard to believe, progress was still being made.

Although it was hard, Mariko continued to work on her feelings about the attack and related issues. She began to see why she had difficulty trusting her fiancé, why she had the need to "always be on guard, always ready to either fight or run."

Unfortunately, the more she dealt with it, the more depressed she became. It had opened up "a Pandora's box of emotions for me, and I didn't feel like I could cope with it all." About a year into treatment, Mariko was so distraught she began having thoughts of suicide.

Mariko and her therapist decided it was time to consult with a psychiatrist and discuss medication. Her depression had become so severe that she could barely get out of bed in the morning and she was finding it hard to concentrate on anything. "Somehow I managed to keep up with my job, but it took "all I had just to hold it together."

Mariko saw a psychiatrist who agreed that drug therapy might be helpful. She began taking an antidepressant and made another appointment with the psychiatrist for follow-up. As the medication began to take effect, Mariko felt better able to cope.

> *It didn't solve everything, but it did get me out of bed and back into my life. I was willing to look at my issues again. It also gave me some relief and hope.*

With the help of her treatment team, family, and friends, Mariko was eventually able to fully come to terms with having been raped. As she worked through the emotions, thoughts, and beliefs related to that trauma and came to understand their connection to her bulimia, she was able to decrease her bingeing and purging. It wasn't always easy; she found herself being "pulled" to binge often, but she was increasingly able to find other ways of handling her feelings.

At this point, Mariko was bingeing and purging twice a week on average, an enormous reduction from when she had begun treatment. Although her goal was eventually to discontinue medication, she stayed on it during this phase, as both she and her psychiatrist felt it was still helpful for her. She was committed to continuing her work on overcoming the eating disorder, and she was proud of the fact that after nine years of bingeing and purging three to five times per day, she was on the road to recovery.

For Mariko, this marked the end of phase two, which lasted about two years. She felt the event and issues that fueled the bulimia had been thoroughly dealt with and she had her eating-disordered behavior under control.

> *It wasn't that everything was perfect, I mean, I still had work to do, I still threw up sometimes, but I could finally devote my energy to living life instead of just being bulimic.*

## Phase Three: Reclaiming Her Life

Getting through the first two stages of treatment and recovery is a real achievement. As difficult and intense as these phases can be, they do offer a kind of simplicity and clarity because the focus is on treatment and recovery.

In the third phase of treatment, however, your loved one needs to balance many different things in addition to her new relationship with food. She may be going to school, working at a job, being a wife or mother, increasing exercise, or spending more time with friends. These can be wonderful, fulfilling activities, but they can complicate her efforts to stay on task. Thus, the challenge of this final stage of treatment is for your loved one to achieve a healthy equilibrium among all the different aspects of her new and full life.

Phase three has three principal and interrelated goals. The first is for your loved one to maintain what has been accomplished in the previous two stages; for instance, keeping her weight in an appropriate range or relying on other ways of coping than bingeing or purging. The second is to develop the kind of life she wants for herself by resuming activities she engaged in before the onset of the eating disorder or by pursuing new interests. The third goal of this phase is to learn to be fully involved and engaged in her life without falling back into the eating disorder.

People have differing views regarding when an eating disorder is considered "over" or "resolved." Some people believe an individual who has anorexia or bulimia has it for life. This perspective has its roots in addiction theory and treatment—once in recovery always in recovery. Others believe it is possible to be healed completely, with no residual desire to return to old behaviors. At some level, however, debate about whether an eating disorder is a lifelong proposition is a semantic or technical one: all sides of the discussion would likely agree that recovery is a process—one that requires ongoing attention and self-care in a variety of ways for varying lengths of time.

The rewards of phase three are numerous. At this point, the eating disorder no longer consumes her every thought, and your loved one has the freedom and peace of mind that was missing when the illness was at its most intense. In addition, she is better able to accept that she is a valuable person, regardless of her body size. Furthermore, relationships with both herself and others have begun to take precedence over her relationship with the eating disorder.

In terms of treatment itself, the goal of this phase is to gradually decrease the frequency of her various appointments. As your loved one becomes more confident in her abilities, she will be better able to deal with life autonomously, solve her own dilemmas, and comfort and reassure herself. At some point she becomes so practiced at these things that she can consistently accomplish them without assistance from her treatment team.

When and how to accomplish the decrease in treatment is a matter for your loved one and her team to decide. There is no one right way to do it. The important thing is for her to receive continuous support and assistance as long as she needs and wants it.

Let's take a final look at Karen and Mariko and see how they handled this last phase of treatment.

## Karen's Recovery—Phase Three

When Karen was finally ready to return to college, she was at the point where she needed only a monthly medical check-up and a single weekly visit to her therapist. She had also decreased appointments with the dietitian to every other week. These were not overnight changes, and Karen needed a period of adjustment for each one

> *Each time we changed something, even when it was my idea and I wanted it, it was scary. I would worry about what would happen and if I was going to be okay. But I trusted my team wouldn't let me do anything they thought I couldn't handle.*

Returning to school turned out to be particularly stressful due to the long days and constant homework. And, although she had missed her schoolmates, she also felt awkward being around them again.

*I didn't really know what to tell them or how to talk to them about what I'd been doing. My closest ones already knew, of course, since I'd talked to them, even when I was in the hospital. Other people only knew I had left school. I didn't know what to say.*

More than anything, Karen continued to have nagging feelings of failure. Not only had she succumbed to an eating disorder, she had quit school and abandoned her friends for over a year.

*I sort of thought I failed and disappointed my parents by taking time off. They kept telling me they were just glad that I was healthy enough to get back to my life. But I still worried. I worried about that with my friends, too. Did they think I was a loser? Were they disappointed in me for leaving school?*

Karen had to keep on task when it came to balancing school and her recovery, but doing so proved her desire and commitment to get better.

*It was easy to skip meals when I had a class to go to or lots of studying to do. I had to pay close attention to eating enough, and that was annoying, but I knew I had to do it if I wanted to get through school in one piece.*

*I stumbled sometimes, but I think most people probably do. It helped to be reminded that I didn't have to be perfect at recovering from anorexia.*

Once Karen settled into the routine of college life and all its demands, enjoying meals with adequate nutrition and variety became easier and easier. By the spring semester, she could go to most restaurants with her friends and could always find something she felt comfortable ordering. Her weight continued to remain within a healthy range, and she was able to engage in adequate, not excessive, exercise.

During summer break, Karen got a job as a camp counselor about 100 miles from her family home.

*At first I worried about being away from home and about having to eat whatever the camp offered. At the same time, I wanted to do it. I thought*

*I could handle most things that might happen there, and if not, I could
always come home.*

As with everything else, working at camp proved to be a challenge that
required a period of adjustment. However, Karen relied on everything she
had learned during recovery and was able to stay on track and healthy
throughout the summer.

*It was amazing that I could have such a good time, that I wasn't obsessing
about food or weight hardly at all.*

Soon after returning from camp Karen began the next school year, and felt
ready to leave treatment entirely.

*I hadn't been in treatment all summer, and things had gone really well. I
knew if I ever needed to, or just wanted to, I could always call my team.*

After the termination of her treatment, Karen continued to do well. Managing the disorder became less and less of a concern, and she felt like she
was developing a life she wanted for herself. When she encountered a
stressful event or uncomfortable emotion, Karen sometimes felt the "pull
of the anorexia calling me to come back, like it wanted to help me feel
more secure." In times like these, she focused on taking care of herself and
getting the support she needed.

*Sometimes talking to friends or family was enough, but sometimes I
thought it would be good to just check in with my therapist about what was
going on. So I'd call her.*

After obtaining her undergraduate degree, she entered graduate school
in another state, feeling ready and eager to take on this new challenge.
Although she missed her family and experienced the usual fears of a new
situation, Karen was finally in charge of her life.

## Mariko's Recovery—Phase Three

Late in the second year of treatment Mariko's life was full of changes. She married her fiancé, changed jobs, and moved into a bigger house with her new husband. She still valued therapy and was willing to make time for it despite her busy schedule.

> *I sometimes still had trouble dealing with my feelings without using binge-ing and purging, but each time I did, I felt very proud, like it reinforced that I could do this.*

Mariko was gradually able to decrease her bingeing and purging to once a week at most. "If I had a particularly stressful week, I might binge more frequently, but in general I did it less and less over time."

She continued weekly sessions with her therapist and consulted with the dietitian once a month. Because her physical health was so improved, she only needed to see her physician every six to eight weeks.

About a year after getting married, Mariko became pregnant. When she began to binge and purge daily and feel "disgusted and disappointed" in herself, she knew she needed to address the situation.

> *We had been trying for several months, and we were so excited that it finally worked. Since I wanted it so much, I didn't think about the fact that it might affect my recovery. I didn't anticipate my reaction. I suddenly felt freaked out, like I was going to get fat, like I was out of control, and like my body was out to get me. I was terrified.*

In order to avoid any problems with the baby, Mariko made an effort to see her therapist, dietitian, and physician more frequently during this time. The team worked together to help her understand why being pregnant was making her so anxious and to help her reduce the disordered eating.

> *I could see how, despite truly wanting this baby, becoming pregnant had triggered some of those old feelings from having been attacked.*

She felt that "somehow I was infected or unclean, and that made me want to throw up." She also recognized that having a baby growing inside her made her feel out of control, and she needed help to "trust that the baby was not an adversary and that it was not going to hurt me in any way."

As Mariko worked through these matters, her anxiety decreased, and so did the need for the bingeing and purging. She again got the bulimia under control and felt strong and proud of herself.

After giving birth to a healthy baby, Mariko went through another adjustment—*motherhood*. She knew she needed support to allay doubts as to whether she'd be a good enough mom. She also feared she wouldn't be able to protect her child, just the way she couldn't protect herself when she had been attacked as a teenager.

She worked on these issues in therapy, and they became easier to manage. Sometimes her husband joined her so he could better understand what she was going through and how to help and support her.

As the baby grew, Mariko "felt more confident in my ability to be a good mother." By the time the baby turned two, Mariko found herself bingeing and purging only rarely, maybe once every five or six months or so, which was a vast reduction from the three to five times per day when she began treatment.

At this point, Mariko felt she was in a place of maintenance in terms of her eating disorder. "I still hoped that there would be a point where I would never binge and purge again," and she intended to continue working toward that goal. She felt she was really living her life now, and that the eating disorder no longer dominated her every moment like it had for so many years.

**CHAPTER 8**

# Supporting Her Recovery

## *How Can I Help?*

Over and over, families tell us they want to help with their loved one's recovery, but they don't know what to do. They know they can't fix her eating disorder, because only she can do that. But there are things that they *can* do that are supportive and constructive. Something as basic as taking care of *their* health so that they remain strong and present to the needs of their loved one can be of tremendous help. So can the simple acts of listening carefully or speaking honestly. In this chapter we list several ways you can best help with the recovery process.

## Learn About Eating Disorders

Of primary importance is becoming educated about the illness. Read books or blogs, browse reputable websites, or talk to therapists or other families who have gone through recovery (see Helpful Organizations for recommendations). Knowledge gives you power and, based on the information you gather, you can make well-informed decisions about how to proceed. In addition, your loved one will likely be grateful that you care enough to learn about her condition.

*We thought eating disorders were only about food. We had no idea they were about emotions.*

*Meeting with our own therapist allowed us to get our questions answered. As we learned about our daughter's illness we were finally able to truly help, not just get in her way.*

*I thought my job was to make her eat. It took a long time and a lot of different people to get me to understand my job was to listen and to help her be a stronger and more confident young woman.*

## Talk to Her

How can you talk to your loved one in ways that have the best chance of being understood and heard? The fact is that you are in a challenging position. On the one hand, you want to communicate that you're supportive and want to be of assistance. On the other, you may feel frustrated or angry about her behaviors, or even want to "shake some sense into her." Sometimes family and friends feel like they are "walking on eggshells" around their loved one. After all, they don't want to make things worse or alienate her, so they avoid saying what they really feel or think.

One key to effective communication with someone with an eating disorder is to remind yourself that your loved one sees her illness as a vital, indispensable friend. If you speak about it in disparaging terms, she might get defensive, think you don't understand her, or that you don't care. She will likely feel threatened, as if you're trying to take away something she needs to survive. For these reasons, be calm and caring when you express your worry about how the disorder is affecting her, and let her know how frightened you are.

Remember that proper timing, choice of words, and the *way* in which you say something are essential to positive communication. Pick a place where food or eating is not involved and a time when tensions are low between the two of you. For example, a family holiday dinner is typically *not* the best occasion to express your concerns! Opportunities might best be found in a location that feels neutral, such as shopping at the mall, hiking in the mountains, or watching a movie at home, so she won't feel "cornered," "ambushed," or "set up." You'll meet with more success if you're both having a good time and feeling relaxed.

Be thoughtful and careful when you speak. Talk to her in a steady voice about the way *you* experience or feel about her illness. Using "I" statements (such as "I feel . . . " or "I am worried. . . ") will give you the best chance of being heard. For instance, you might say, "I am concerned about you and worried about your health" rather than, "You are killing yourself and I want you to stop it right now!" The latter is a confrontation, not a conversation and, instead of opening the lines of communication and bonding with your loved one, might create misunderstanding and distance.

Speaking in the first person and keeping your emotions at bay while thinking through what you want to say can prove to be difficult for some individuals. Sometimes you may become so fretful or exhausted you may feel like you're going to implode. Expressing your feelings while trying to understand hers can be a difficult balancing act, but it's integral to good communication. Don't expect your first efforts to be perfect, but do keep trying.

Think about what you most want to convey and try to be gentle yet specific. Remember how sensitive she is to feeling criticized and thinking she's inadequate. Choose your tone and words wisely. Over time, with patience and a deepened understanding of the relationship she has with her eating disorder, you'll both be able to speak more freely, which will help strengthen her relationships with you, other people, and herself.

Remind her often that you're available to listen, to do things with her, and to generally support her in any way she can think of. Sometimes she won't know or be able to articulate what would be helpful to her at the moment. That's okay, and you can tell her so. Asking what she needs every once in while will demonstrate you really are there for her and have not disappeared, grown tired of the situation, or abandoned her.

> *I'd sometimes blow it and blurt out things that sounded mean or angry. I knew it as they came out of my mouth, but I couldn't always help it. After awhile we made a deal: she could hold up her hand and tell me I needed a time out to think about what I was saying, and we'd both take a break for a few minutes and then try again. It was hard to get used to, but it worked.*

> *I had so much I wanted to say to her. I was so afraid for her. I didn't want to scare her, though, or make things worse. So, I didn't ever say anything.*

> *It was frustrating. I wasn't sure what was okay to say and what wasn't. I didn't want to hurt her feelings, but I also didn't want to lie and pretend I didn't have any feelings of my own about what was going on with her.*

## Be and Stay Aware

As you know, an eating disorder develops gradually, almost imperceptibly, and often leaves you wondering if your suspicions are real or unfounded. The same is true of recovery: it is a gradual process with milestones and pitfalls that are sometimes hard to recognize or measure.

Keep your eyes open for subtle changes in your loved one's relationships with herself, friends and family, and food and eating. Praise positive steps while remaining mindful of the possibility of relapse. Try not to doubt yourself if you notice or suspect she is losing ground, but at the same time don't make assumptions. The best course is to avoid second-guessing the situation by talking to her calmly and directly. Explain what you've observed and express your concerns for her health and wellbeing.

> *I thought she had begun to restrict her food again. I was very afraid of what might come next. I finally talked to her, and she said she had noticed the same thing and was working on it with her therapist.*

*I was sure she had lost weight. When I got up the courage to say something she told me to ask her doctor. It turned out she had grown an inch and her weight was fine. I was glad I got the information and didn't just assume things.*

*She started being less social again. I was worried it was the eating disorder coming back. We talked about it and she said she felt like she had outgrown her friends, that the things they were interested in no longer were what she was interested in, so she wasn't hanging out with them as much. I was glad. I was relieved it was a sign of growth, not a step backwards.*

If she is heading towards relapse, assess the situation and make decisions accordingly. Your strategy for what to do next, if anything, will depend on a variety of factors, including her age and whether or not she appears to be in immediate medical danger. If you do elect to take action, discuss your observations and apprehensions with her first, and let her know you feel it's necessary for you to intervene for the sake of her health. Although such a conversation might not be comfortable for either of you, it will allow you to convey your concerns and demonstrate that you aren't going to do anything "behind her back."

## Break Through the Secrecy

Your loved one may feel so compelled to use the disordered-eating behaviors that she will continue to try to prevent anyone from discovering them, and therefore possibly taking them away. For this reason, she may go to great lengths to assure what she is doing remains a secret. In support of her recovery, you will need to understand the intensity of this need to hide the illness.

When the time feels right, communicate that you understand how difficult and frightening what she's going through must be. Let her know you are neither mad at nor disappointed in her. Make it clear that you don't consider her weak because she developed an eating disorder and that you don't expect her to have an instant recovery. Treating your loved one in such a fashion will help keep her from trying to do things "perfectly" while in treatment. It will also encourage her to open up and be honest about her emotions and what she's thinking. By offering your support and empathy, she will be more able to let go of the secrecy because she will no longer fear your judgment or reprimand.

> *I couldn't have been more surprised by the way she thinks. What she's afraid I think about her is so off-base.*

> *I was afraid to tell her what I thought because I was worried I'd hurt her feelings. She was worried I thought she'd failed me and her mom.*

> *Once I started talking to her, I mean after awhile, she finally started telling me what she really was freaked out about.*

## Listen

Listening can't be emphasized enough, since someone with an eating disorder tends to feel deeply misunderstood, as though people don't appreciate or care about what she's going through. Simply being available to listen impartially to your loved one when she has something to explain or confess is one of the greatest gifts you can offer.

This may not always be as easy as it sounds. Sometimes she may say things that are hard to understand, frighten you, or make you angry or disgusted. But if you could learn to set aside your judgments and give her your undivided attention, she'll see you *do* care and want her to get well. This will in turn increase her self-esteem and desire to recover.

> *I didn't need them to fix anything, I knew I had to do that myself, but they seemed to feel it was their responsibility to do something. What would have been the best is for them to ask how I was, what I was thinking, what was going on with me.*

> *I really wanted to just talk to them. I didn't even know what I wanted to say. I wanted them to hear me.*

*My mom and dad finally sat me down and asked me what was happening, what I was doing to myself. It was really hard, but I told them, and they were great. They didn't make me feel like I was bad or gross. I could tell they wanted to help, just to find out what I wanted.*

## Help Her Get Support

One major factor that affects an individual's rate of recovery is the amount of support she has. In general, the more support, the better. Recovery can feel very lonely at times. Having people she can rely on, a pet to play with and take care of, or hobbies where she interacts with others can make a big difference. Anything that interests and engages her or increases her sense of intimacy or belonging can help keep her motivated in her pursuit of recovery.

Since she is unique, the types of support she'll find most valuable will depend on her personality and interests. Beneficial activities can range from caring for animals, pursuing art, music, or writing classes, to volunteering for charitable organizations.

*I didn't even think I liked animals, but my therapist convinced me to get a cat. Until I had the confidence to make friends with human beings that cat was my best friend. My relationship with him showed me I could actually have relationships, that someone could really love me.*

*I started going to church every week. I hadn't been in years. I found a great community there, and I got my relationship back with God.*

## Acknowledge Your Emotions

Being in a relationship with someone who has an eating disorder can be many things, including worrisome, confusing, frustrating, and maddening. After all, your loved one is endangering her health and life. Don't be surprised if you have some pretty strong emotions about the situation. This is normal. What's more, there may be times when you don't have the energy or patience to really be there for her. That's normal, too. A full range of reactions is to be expected and can be managed.

Getting some help for yourself, such as counseling or joining a group for parents, is recommended. Any kind of therapy or support group gives you the chance to ask questions about and get assistance with your own emotions. You can explore in-depth how your loved one's eating disorder makes you feel and to learn to confront these emotions in healthy and constructive ways. Groups afford a particular benefit: you get to hear other parents speak about their experiences and the ways in which they deal with them, and you can be reminded you aren't alone in what you feel.

Connecting with your emotions has several benefits. For one thing, it allows you to stay connected to your loved one. For example, if you are trying *not* to feel angry or scared, you won't be able to pay attention to what she is saying or how you might want to respond to her words. You'll be distracted and stymied by your efforts to pretend that you are calm when you are not. This will only cause your loved one to become suspicious or untrusting.

Additionally, you are a crucial role model for your loved one. She needs to see you can experience a wide range of emotions without becoming overwhelmed, something she is much of the time. If you act as though you don't feel such things as frustration or fear, she'll follow your lead and try to deny or rid herself of these kinds of emotions. A major aspect of her recovery is learning to believe she can tolerate and survive her feelings. She needs to observe people successfully doing this very thing.

Finally, discounting, dismissing or attempting to eradicate emotions is unhealthy and can lead to physical and/or personal problems down the road. If you don't acknowledge and try to stifle what you truly feel at any given moment, your emotions can fester like an infection. Eventually, they will erupt, sometimes in unexpected and painful ways.

> *So many emotions came up in me and in the rest of our family. We weren't sure if that was normal. We had no one to talk to about it. We all felt bad, like maybe we were betraying her by having our own feelings and reactions about her illness.*

*It finally felt like we were real. For years we had all tiptoed around, like we were plastic models or something. Like we didn't feel anything. It took my daughter's anorexia to break us out of that. Now we feel connected to each other. It doesn't mean everything's always happy, but it does mean we always get to be real.*

*My emotions were all over the place. One minute I wanted to scream. The next minute I wanted to cry. Then give up. Then hold her. It felt so crazy.*

## Take Care of Yourself

The need to maintain your personal health cannot be stressed enough. If you aren't doing well, you will be of no use to yourself or your loved one. Devoting all your attention, time, and energy to dealing with her illness may work during a momentary crisis or for very short periods of time, but it won't work for the long haul.

You're going to need maximum strength and patience to be there for her as she recovers. Take time for yourself and your needs, have some fun, and make sure your other relationships remain healthy. You need to set an example by living a rich, full, and happy life. Put yourself first when it is appropriate! And don't be shy about asking members of your loved one's treatment team for ideas or recommendations, as well as comfort.

Just as your loved one needs a strong support system, you do, too. Friends and family can be of tremendous value, as can professionals, such as therapists, social workers, and clergy. Additionally, sharing stories with other parents who have gone through or are going through similar experiences, either in person, on the telephone, or online, can help sustain you and provide encouragement and hope.

*I thought it meant I was a bad mom if I did anything for myself while she was ill. I thought it meant I didn't care.*

*I just felt I needed to be there for her all the time. It didn't matter what I felt like or what I wanted. I thought I had to give everything to her, but it ended up wearing me out.*

*Our daughter's therapist told us we had to do things for fun. I thought she was kidding. Who could have fun at a time like this? But she turned out to be right.*

*I gave up everything else I was doing: friends, entertaining, took time off from work, you name it. And you know what? It didn't even help. I mean, I know she was grateful that I tried, but she felt smothered and I felt exhausted and resentful.*

## Focus on Life Beyond the Illness

Anorexia or bulimia impacts not only the life of the person who has the illness, but the lives of her entire family and social group. It's not hard to see how this happens. After all, having an eating disorder is a serious matter. You want your loved one to know you care and that you're trying to help her, but not to such a degree that your lives are consumed by it.

Sometimes, doing things together and talking about subjects that are completely unrelated is extremely beneficial. There is life beyond the eating disorder! Not focusing on it exclusively is especially important, since she can so easily believe she *is* her illness. Furthermore, this will show that you aren't overwhelmed or devastated by her symptoms, that you are able to maintain a life *and* help her create one *without* her disease.

*All we would talk about was the bulimia. It was like there wasn't anything else in our lives. We had to learn, or re-learn maybe, to make ourselves talk about and do other things.*

*I didn't realize she wanted me to do other things. I thought she wanted me to sit around all day with her and to act sad and worried, both of which I of course was. She finally told me that what really helped her was for us to go about our regular life. She didn't like all the attention just on her. It made it harder to eat.*

*It was hard to remember we could have fun and be happy, even though we had a daughter who was ill. The more we did, though, the better she seemed.*

## Encourage Authenticity

An individual who develops an eating disorder tends to be high functioning and high achieving, someone who rarely looks or acts as insecure as she truly feels. Watch carefully for signs she is attempting to look "together" or "fine" when she might not be feeling either of those, and invite her to talk to you about what's going on for her.

Don't try to convince her that what she is feeling is false, imagined, or insignificant. In other words, pay close attention to and honor what is emotionally true or authentic *for her*. In this way, you are helping her develop a strong sense of who she is, what she believes, and what is important to her. Remind her that she is loved for who she *is*, not for what she does or how she looks. Encourage her to participate in activities because she truly enjoys them, not to please someone else or because she thinks she is "supposed to."

Also assure her that no one is "together" all the time, and that perfection is neither possible nor the point of life. It's important to have and attain goals, but what she does or does not achieve doesn't define her as a person or make her any more lovable.

Remember, she'll be watching and wanting you to demonstrate how living without an eating disorder can work. Model ways to love and appreciate your own body. Honor your feelings. Work to improve your relationships. Be honest. In these and many other ways unique to your family, you will teach her that even though life is full of challenges, she will be able to develop strategies and find resources to handle them.

*I knew I could recover. Well, most of the time I knew it. I guess my family knew it also, because they never gave up. And I'm truly grateful. They kept hanging in there, even when it was tough. It took a long time, but I finally made it. We all did.*

# Helpful Organizations

ANAD National Association of Anorexia Nervosa and Associated Disorders
*www.anad.org,* 847-831-3438
PO Box 7, Highland Park, IL 60035
Provides a crisis hotline and maintains a list of providers and treatment facilities.

NEDA National Eating Disorders Association
*www.nationaleatingdisorders.org,* 800-931-2237
603 Stewart St., Suite 803, Seattle, WA 98101
This organization is dedicated to expanding public understanding of eating disorders and promoting access to treatment and support to family and loved ones.

Gürze Books
*www.bulimia.com,* 800-756-7533
PO Box 2238, Carlsbad, CA 92018
Provides information about eating disorders, including books, newsletters, a therapist directory, links to treatment facilities, author blogs, and much more.

# About the Authors

## Johanna Marie McShane, PhD

Dr. Johanna Marie Mcshane has been working in the field of eating disorders treatment for eighteen years. She was staff therapist and assessment/intake counselor for the Serenity Eating Disorders Program at Mt. Diablo Medical Center, an inpatient eating disorders program in Northern California, from 1991 to 1994. She was a founding member and director of psychotherapies at the Integrated Therapies Program for Eating Disorders, an intensive outpatient program also in Northern California, from 1996 to 1998. Dr. McShane has been in private practice since 1994, working with adolescents and adults who have eating disorders, their families and significant others. She is co-developer of the Diablo Valley Family Centered Model, a psychotherapeutic treatment model for working with families in which there is an eating disorder or related issue.

In addition to working directly with patients, Dr. McShane leads seminars for professionals and facilitates workshops for people who suffer from eating disorders. She has spoken extensively about causes and treatment of anorexia, bulimia and binge-eating disorders, and regularly provides consultation for clinics, hospitals and private practitioners. She has published in *Eating Disorders: The Journal of Treatment and Prevention*, *Eating Disorders Today*, *The Journal of Trauma and Dissociation*, and other publications, and has made numerous television and radio appearances speaking about eating disorders.

# Tony Paulson, PhD

Dr. Tony Paulson holds a bachelor's degree in psychology and a master's degree in social work, both from Sacramento State University. He earned his doctorate at Saybrook Graduate School in San Francisco, where he received the Charles Thuss Award for exceptional writing and research, based on his work in eating disorders.

More than 17 years ago, Dr. Paulson began treating people suffering from anorexia and bulimia nervosa. He quickly discovered a passion for this population, and a great desire to contribute in a meaningful way to the understanding of these disorders in an effort to alleviate the tremendous suffering these patients endure. Early in his career, he committed himself to providing compassionate, effective treatment, and to increasing patient and family understanding of what anorexia and bulimia are all about.

Dr. Paulson currently serves as Clinical Director for Summit Eating Disorders Program, an Intensive Outpatient Program and Day Treatment Program serving Northern California. Dr. Paulson lectures extensively on the topic of eating disorders on state and national levels, and frequently lectures to community groups throughout California.

# About the Publisher

Since 1980, Gürze Books has been dedicated to providing quality information on eating disorders recovery, research, education, advocacy, and prevention. They publish *Eating Disorders Today*, a newsletter for individuals in recovery and their loved ones, and the *Eating Disorders Review*, a clinical newsletter for professionals. The company also widely distributes the *Eating Disorders Resource Catalogue*, and has two helpful websites, *www.bulimia.com* and *www.eatingdisordersblogs.com*.

# Order at *www. bulimia. com*
# Or by phone 1-800-756-7533

*Why She Feels Fat* is available at bookstores and libraries and may be ordered directly from the Gürze Books website, *www.bulimia.com,* or by phone 1-800-756-7533.

## FREE Catalogue

The *Eating Disorders Resource Catalogue* features books on eating and weight-related topics, including body image, size acceptance, self-esteem and more. It also includes listings of nonprofit associations and treatment facilities and is handed out by therapists, educators, and other health care professionals around the world. Visit *www.bulimia.com* to request free copies.

## Eating Disorders Today

The *Eating Disorders Today* newsletter is a compassionate and supportive publication for individuals in recovery and their loved ones. It combines helpful facts and self-help advice from experts in the field. Quarterly subscriptions available. Request a sample issue at *www.bulimia.com.*

## *www.bulimia.com*

Visit our website for additional resources, including many free articles, hundreds of books, and links to organizations, treatment facilities and other websites.

## *www.eatingdisordersblogs.com*

*EatingDisordersBlogs.com* is a website with author blogs for connecting with others about food and feelings, healthy eating, family concerns, and recovery issues.